× £4.50

FOUR YE
DEATH OF THE

C000292032

FOUR YEARS
IN THE DEATH
OF THE
LABOUR PARTY

Austin Mitchell

METHUEN

To Jonathan

First published in Great Britain 1983
by Methuen London Ltd
11 New Fetter Lane, London EC4P 4EE
Copyright © 1983 Austin Mitchell

Printed in Great Britain by
Redwood Burn Limited, Trowbridge

ISBN 0 413 54570 9 hardback
0 413 54550 4 paperback

*This book is available in both
hardback and paperback editions.
The paperback is sold subject to the condition
that it shall not, by way of trade or otherwise,
be lent, resold, hired out, or otherwise circulated
without the publisher's prior consent in any form
of binding or cover other than that in which
it is published and without a similar condition
including this condition being imposed
upon the subsequent purchaser.*

Contents

Preface

Acknowledgements

My thanks to the numerous interviewees who provided the facts and don't wish to be associated with the conclusions. Several colleagues, parliamentary, pedagogic and practical, read through the manuscript. They know who they are. Since listing them looks self-important and could embarrass, I have decided to drop names rather than name-drop. Anne Holgeth, Jenny Bristow, Sally Jenner and Margaret Wheatley decoded the Linear B of my script into type. Adrian Barker, Ginger Knox, Gair McCullough and Joan Carrellas did the research and my minder Micky Chittenden kept us at it and the world at bay.

AUSTIN MITCHELL
Grimsby, July 1983

1 · The Non-election of 1983

'It is not enough to create a programme, it is necessary that the working class accept it. But the sectarian, in the nature of things, comes to a full stop upon half the task.'
LEON TROTSKY

'It was a larger victory than I dared hope for' Margaret Thatcher said of the 1983 election. Her minions in the press also portrayed it as 'a resounding personal triumph for Margaret Hilda Thatcher, 57, the grocer's daughter from Grantham' (*Time*). 'Landslide for the Tories' said the *Daily Telegraph*, 'Triumphant Maggie is swept back' chorused the *Star* while the *Sun* dubbed it 'the Maggie Massacre', a reference not to her kindnesses to the wets but to the Prime Minister 'storming to a huge victory in the General Election'. She didn't. The 'vote of confidence' was a 3 per cent drop in the proportion of the British electorate voting Conservative to a lower share than Sir Alex Douglas-Home had managed in 1964. Thanks to the perversities of a first-past-the-post electoral system articulating three major parties this timid rebuff was alchemised into a Tory majority of 144, mostly identikit Thatcherites or Central Office clones with no new thoughts to offer on old problems. When, immediately after the election, the economic price of winning it had to be paid and the sky blackened with chickens coming home to roost, the more astute, some of them Tories, asked the obvious question. Was it worthwhile going to such great lengths for such a grudging verdict? The election was not necessary for a year. Better to be seen doing duty than to look like deceiving the electorate.

The people did not choose Conservatism. They rejected Labour. The most decisive rejection of any political party since Labour in 1931 or the Conservatives in 1945. Yet they were governments in power. Now, with unemployment at a real figure of over four million, output down to the level of 1967, the electorate was punishing the opposition. Labour lost 9.5 per cent of its vote, 8.2 per cent of the population qualified to vote and 119 deposits, which was one in five seats fought and half as much again as all the deposits lost in all the eleven previous elections by Labour. It was driven into third or fourth place in 292 seats. Its share of the vote was lower than in 1922, its vote per candidate lower than the 1900s when the infant party first came on to the political stage, squalling and mewling then too. Even the most highly publicised aspect of the election, the rise of the Alliance of Liberals and SDP to a quarter of the votes, the best third party vote for sixty years, was really only a reflection and a by-product of what had happened to Labour. The Alliance attracted two people from Labour for every one from the Conservatives.

For the first time the opposition was the election issue, not the government. Everything that followed, the Labour slippage, the Alliance surge, the nature of the campaign, was about that. The election, therefore, requires study not through the conventional analysis of government decision-making, the campaign, the polls and media reactions, but in terms of its dominant pattern: Labour's demise. What happened to the party was not a sudden loss of faith but the end of a long process of decline and disintegration. This is the story of four years in the death of Labour's aspiration to be the natural party of government. A once great party, a party which formed the government for half the post-war period up to 1979, was reduced to a rump.

Labour lost because it didn't get enough votes. Explaining why is more difficult. It is not a scientific process: much can be asserted, little proved. The evidence indicates that the death was *felo de se*, not a who-dunnit. Yet there is a balance sheet to be drawn between free will in its Labour manifestation of inept decisions, accidental results, human fallibility and incompetence, particularly on the part of people whose hearts were always in the right place, and, on the other hand, historical inevitability in which everyone plays a conditioned role, stumbling like sleepwalkers to an inevitable disaster.

If predestination plays the bigger part, the story is a chapter in Britain's decline. Since the war the country has passed through the politics of affluence, entrenching the Tory party of 'You've never had it so good' in power for thirteen years, then the politics of uncertainty, producing more and more rapid changes of government party, and within each government changes of policy, than in any other comparable country. In the 1970s the rest of the advanced world followed Britain into this phase of uncertainty. The result was that the only western leaders re-elected since the oil crisis broke in 1973 have been Malcolm Fraser, beaten in 1983, Robert Muldoon and Helmut Schmidt, whose precarious coalition collapsed in two years.

As this happened Britain had already moved ahead into a new phase, leading the world politically by lagging economically. That phase – still dominant – is the politics of decline. Her decline had long been comparative. After a time the gap produced by comparative decline becomes so wide, industries and markets so exposed, that things must turn down; decline becomes absolute. That point came earlier than it otherwise might because of the combined impact of oil price crises, world depression and the masochistic belief, implicit in Thatchernomics, that things have to be made worse before they can be made better. They duly were. Both parties had competed and manoeuvred to take power when Britain became self-sufficient in oil. The benefits were assumed to be enormous, entrenching whichever party presided over it in power for decades. Under Thatchernomics its consequences were ruinous because it came on stream only to amplify the disastrous effects of perverse economic policies. Instead of being used to regenerate industry and expand the economy through balance of payment difficulties, oil became the agent of decline, financing manufactured imports to destroy jobs. Its tax revenues were then used to support the unemployment it had created. With the best prospects in the advanced world, because she alone had such a boon, Britain used it to reinforce decline and fell further, deeper and harder into the pit of depression than any other advanced country just when she should have been climbing out of it. The consequences were disastrous. In theory, decline and misery should radicalise and heighten the previous instability. In an informed pragmatic country, with an expectation of steady improvement and direct democratic power over sensitive politicians, they might. They had radicalised in Anglo-Saxon offshoots in Australia and New Zealand and the United States in the 1930s. Not so in Britain, then or now. Operating in an environment of low expectations, deference and simple prejudice and ignorance, decline can also frighten and divide. Those in work fear for their jobs. They also fear change. A new conservative vested interest is created: those a cut above the rest see the main threat to their comparative well-being as those below, not the way the system is being run by those above. The effect was to end instability by entrenching populist conservatism, generating doubt and fear about the possibility of any alternative, particularly one which was novel. The economics of the 1920s produced a return to the politics of that era too.

The electorate was conditioned by economic depression. So was the opposition. The new men, those who came forward with new answers, were but a simple product of depression and the failure and discredit of existing men, conventional solutions. The party of progress gets frustrated when progress is slow. The party of change leaps to the conclusion that by changing itself it can pave the way for change in society. So depression conditioned the behaviour of those who sought to end it, even to the extent of rendering them incapable of doing that very job, thus locking the country into her decline. The policies necessary to cope with decline are harder and stronger than those appropriate to temperate times. As such they are less acceptable to an electorate frightened by decline itself.

What happened was also a product of free will, a DIY disaster, the product of choices, mistakes, blunders and simple silliness, all working in the same direction as the binding depression. Jim Callaghan mistimed the 1979 election and alienated the unions, leading to the collapse of the relationship on which his only political strength was based. The party mishandled the demands for reform, appeasing where they should have stood firm. The catalogue of union ineptitude, absences, mistakes and simple incompetence in the casting of

crucial votes is a long one. In the face of a determined organised campaign, inattention and inadequacy were disastrous.
The lumbering dinosaur was tripped up, tied and fitted with
blinkers. It was then turned loose on what some supposed to
be the pathway to power but which turned out to be a scree
slope to disaster.

At each crisis the party heaved a sigh of relief: things could
not get worse, there was nowhere now to go but up. At each
it found by a kind of Sod's law that things not only could get
worse but did, until the final disaster of Her Majesty's opposition retaining second place by two percentage points, rescu-
ing disaster from the jaws of defeat. It then sighed again and
announced that things could not get worse.

Some defeats were irreversible. The decline of the split
Liberal Party in 1918, and the rejection of its Herculean
effort at revival in 1929, were both milestones on the march
to oblivion. Other defeats become a source of learning, the
prelude to victory. Labour learned from the defeat of 1959
and a modernised revisionist party won in 1964 and, trium-
phantly, in 1966. The 1972 defeat of the childrens'-crusade
radicalism of McGovern's Democratic campaign was the
prelude to restructuring of the party and a new realism which
produced Carter's victory in 1976. Failure in 1945 persuaded
the Conservative Party to reform itself, make itself more pre-
sentable, accept the welfare society and come to the country
as a party of caring and opportunity in 1950.

1983 holds elements of both. Decline is far gone, though
not as far as that of the Liberals after the First World War.
Labour is perilously poised, no longer a national party but a
party of the declining industrial peripheries of Britain,
largely eliminated from the south outside London. To be in
third place in so much of the country is no springboard for
early recovery, and the climb back has too far to go to be
accomplished in one surge. Learning is inevitable, yet the
shackles are tightly tied, those who tied them are strong and
have no concept of any alternative.

Decline is a self-reinforcing syndrome. Those who might
have alternatives are gone or weakened, those who caused it
become more powerful, those who went along with it more
confused, having given so many hostages to fortune. Worms

who did not turn before find it more difficult when buried in debris. Rows caused much of the problem and escape from the disaster could be as debilitating as imposing the shackles proved in the first place. No established party in British or western European politics has ever been supplanted from the front rank without a party split. Yet even that is not impossible and there are certainly examples of decline into irrelevance, such as the French Communist Party, sinking from a third of the vote to less than a sixth inside its proletarian ghetto. Electorates are becoming more volatile especially in Britain so a jump back is feasible – but so is a bigger transfer to the third party. The fact that it could rise so fast and so far in a first-past-the-post electoral system which normally squeezes out all but the two dominant parties shows just how far discontent with the existing system has gone. True, the government is unlikely to be so lucky or so successful again – the gold crown was tarnished as Mrs Thatcher lowered it on to her head – and there will be ample discontent to fuel opposition as the Thatcher experiment fails. No one can be sure into whose tank it will go. The failure of one established party in government does not necessarily help the other in opposition. It can discredit all established parties. It can generate alienation from the system.

The third party is still there, psychologically boosted if numerically small, already taking advantage of by-elections which favour it much more than general elections because each provides an opportunity for the kind of instant alternative vote system which it has exploited so effectively in the last two years. In two out of three by-elections in Tory seats Labour will start from third place. The SDP can be seen either as a burst balloon or a hovering vulture, and the pundits can't discriminate because whatever SDP intentions – and they can be assumed to be malign towards Labour – circumstances will decide its fate.

Yet so will Labour, and the big problem is whether 1983 is a fatal blow, with rigor mortis setting in and hardening the party in the frozen postures of decline, or whether it can learn the lessons of defeat. This book is a passionate plea which can be given in no other way for Labour to learn and return not to the bad old ways but to a sensible appreciation of its role, not as an ideological party, but as the dynamic of the system, the saviour of the nation, the force for progress. Labour's prime commitment is its responsibilities and they lie not to its activists but to the mass of the people. System, nation and people desperately need it to take up those responsibilities again. Is there life after death is a dramatic way of framing the question, imposed by the title of the book. Yet it is not too great an overstatement in the light of the new beginning, the new understanding, required to break out of the trap.

Labour now has no leeway for mistakes. A crash course of learning the lessons of the past is essential. The prescription for what needs to be done is clear and straightforward. The problem is Labour's will and ability to do it. Even a sudden change of attitudes on the part of those who are institutionally tied to the old is not likely to produce power in one stride when Labour is reduced so far. Thus 1983 looks more like the prelude to the ten-year Reichette than a phoenix-from-ashes routine for Labour. Meanwhile, with the party system deadlocked, Britain's decline will go on. The Conservatives are not likely to be able to reverse their own mistakes even if they can be brought to see them. Economic decline too is self-reinforcing. The levers of the two-party system, always, for all its misuse, the great engine of change in a democratic society, are rusting away as Labour declines and a multi-party system emerges. As opportunities and alternatives slip away it will become more and more difficult to reverse the disaster and rebuild by any processes we would recognise as democratic, let alone to do so by any programme which can be presented to an electorate like Britain's with any prospect of acceptance and success. Chances thrown away do not necessarily come back.

Finally, the luck of politics will determine the individual fates of those involved with the party, not the fanatics who will be happier in the sect they are reducing Labour to, but realists who see Labour as fundamentally right, a great force for good but yet dangerously flawed. Labour men were doomed to apparently permanent opposition in the 1950s, to apparently permanent power in the 1960s. Now they are the flotsam and jetsam in the wreckage. They can joke, 'I don't belong to any organised party – I'm Labour.' Yet people enter the party and its politics for all kinds of reasons: ambition, ideology, the kind of naivety known as a desire to build a better world, identification with Labour's class or trade union role, simple reforming zeal. To pursue any or all of these through the Labour Party in parliament looks misguided. It is not currently a viable instrument for either personal drives or the great principles for which it once catered. Watching a once great, and once lovable, party reduce itself to a faction-ridden rump representing protectionist ghettos rather than the broad sweep of the less well-off it used to serve, a party of blocks, the right posing for the flabby, mindless media or the left for the doctrinaire, prejudiced ideologues, rather than communing with the people – all this has been painful to see, agonising to endure. The fact that Labour has done so much of the damage to itself, making its own problems worse under the pretence of making them better in the most inept, clumsy and incompetent way, makes it all the more painful. Despair at what has been done, impotent anger at being unable either to stop it or get those concerned to see the consequences of their actions, are the kind of bitter frustration that breeds ulcers.

This study will be seen as one of them. It is based on the old-fashioned view that political parties are about power. Those which best apply themselves to getting it, to use on behalf of their people and their principles, best justify their existence. This view may now be outdated and the ideologues may be right. Ideology and bright burning principle may be a nobler guide than pragmatism. To look back may be yearning for a system of politics that is dead. Yet the rational man should prefer facts to theories. There is clearly a public feeling that things cannot go on like this. There is an anti-Tory majority in votes. Therefore something is being frustrated and thwarted if Labour fails, and it is failing, in its responsibilities. What was proposed from 1979 to 1983 was an Alternative Political Strategy. It failed in 1983 and should now be disavowed. Predictable mistakes produced inevitable consequences. Labour's Long March Backwards was an unnecessary exercise in avoidable disaster. It may have been impossible to defeat the Conservative government, particularly after the Falklands. Yet it was not necessary to humiliate ourselves. Nor was it inevitable that a party which is still the only real instrument of social progress, the great and good arm of the people, and the best hope of modernising and saving Britain, should be changed from viable instrument to uncertain prospect.

Pundits always hover above the sweaty reality of people, voiding politics of the passion and the principle. They see the story as drama or comic opera. To be part of it is more tragic. Such feelings are bound to come out. An academic might describe things more calmly. My own corduroy jacket still hangs in my wardrobe, slightly smelly, though not as much as when it was my uniform. Yet academic impartiality is often better concealed partisanship garlanded with statistics. So this study makes no pretence to be other than a politician's view with all the partiality, bloody-mindedness and self-serving of the breed: Butler with more bite, less balance, fewer brains. It is not a proper election study. Yet it is the reality behind an election which was a verdict on four years Hard Labour.

Is it disloyal? From the narrow interests of the rump Labour Party it could be so described. Yet these are the interests of the wreckers and those who have gone along with them making Labour a chair salesman's dream at any point where it was necessary to stand up and be counted. The hard-faced men who have done well out of disaster, the ever-growing fish in a drying-out pool, are not the Labour Party, and telling the truth to such a congregation is as relevant as herpes in heaven. For the real Labour Party, those who vote for it, those who should and those who once did, the people who want change not perfection, who don't like what Margaret Thatcher has done but can't see that as a reason for swallowing an indigestible diet of ideology, telling this story is a matter of duty.

Within the party it will be seen as a right-wing *apologia*. It isn't. No one's views can be oversimplified to the label-trading T-shirt politics to which too much of the party's discussion has been reduced. Wanting Labour to win is neither a right nor a left aspiration. Folly is not an ideology. Those unable to see the difference between pursuing a set of policy aspirations and weakening the machine which carries the people to power deserve to be in the kindergarten sects, not a grown-up party. It will also be seen as sour grapes. Perhaps it is; those who have trodden so many should recognise the process. Yet the aim is to rebuild Labour as a party which can win. To learn from mistakes is an essential part of this. We can only do it by looking honestly at what went wrong, something which can't be done just by speaking out in the internal counsels of the party. There is no propensity yet to listen. There is no format by which the necessary task of persuasion can be undertaken.

To explain to people who need Labour and should be Labour how a party which was once theirs was hijacked is something that can't be done in a conference resolution which they'd never hear of or speak to. It requires the development of a view of party and the political system which they feel incohately but which rump radicals would not understand. Which, therefore, is the higher duty: to accept the terms of debate and the system of thought which have reduced Labour to this pass, jumping through alien hoops only to be rejected anyway, to remain silent and watch the disaster, or to take arms against a sea of ideology, telling the truth so that the real Labour Party may recognise it and realise that all is not lost, what though 1983 be lost? The Labour Party is a machine for carrying the people to power and a voice for betterment in Britain's benighted decline. Unless it serves both purposes it becomes the playway politics of futility.

2 · On the Slipway

*There must be no personal recriminations about the
last four years. The minority Labour government
achieved a great deal that was good.*

TONY BENN

This story of the decline of the Labour Party reached a termi-
nal stage – not necessarily an end – on 9 June 1983. Then it
became dramatically clear how far Labour had fallen from
the natural party of government it had tried to be in the confident expanding years of the 1960s. The people's party no
longer had the people. The signs and symptoms had all been
there before but now it was not polls, the media or a particular constituency which spoke, but the people themselves.
The one thing they said clearly was that they did not particularly like the Labour Party.

The starting point of the decline is more difficult to pin-
point. It was not 3 May 1979 when the last Labour government was thrown out of office in the biggest swing against an
incumbent since the war. All that did was discredit the record
of the government by the fiasco of its end and put Labour in
the exposed situation of opposition. There it has always
looked less attractive than in power, and has compounded its
problems by argument. Basic problems and faults which had
long been apparent, and had become more serious in the
1974–79 government, were exacerbated under the pretence
of making the party more effective. Opposition, normally a
time of renewal and revival, became a degenerative afflic-
tion, not a real cure. Each step took the party further away
from power.

The nature of the Labour Party explains its problems. The
most superficial glance at the benches of the House of Commons indicates the strengths and weaknesses of Britain's par-

ties. Saturnine and better groomed, the Tory benches are the Pioneer Corps of the ranks of privilege and power; essentially a tribe, with all its advantages and disadvantages. As in a tribe, dissent is expressed in code not confrontation, understated not shouted from the roof tops. They follow, even where they shouldn't. Yet they are also easily taken over and transformed by a new chief. A party which had cheered on Heath's boom-and-bust expansionism also applauded, though more generously, Margaret Thatcher's glacial monetarism. It will do the same for whatever successor takes over when she has failed.

To be on the Liberal benches is a statement of angularity pursued professionally, not now nonconformist, just the awkward squad of square pegs dedicated to the perpetual pursuit of round holes, a toil as endless as their eccentricity. Even when Cyril Smith takes his place their bench seats individualists, liberals and Liberals, populist and traditionalist, near Social Democrat, crypto-Tory and those devoted to a professional pavement-pounding so perpetual it has driven out ideas altogether. All these sit together masquerading as a party but really an accidental collection of individualists and anti-governmentalists, not a potential government, whose supporters don't follow them so much as use them to protest. There is no natural Liberal.

The Labour benches house a coalition clear from appearances and the blocks they sit in: workers (mostly aging and portly), trade unionists, ideologues educated above their working-class background, pedagogues representing the pedant revolution and its mannerisms, radical reformers, middle-class intellectuals. Collectively they are the prickly party, inevitably argumentative, implicitly divided. Some come from solid backgrounds which they conceal by radical politics. Most are sprung from or remembering the working class, rather than part of it now, because Labour is hungry, rising and radical, the source of ideas, change and also, in depression, protection for its people.

The parliamentary ranks of the other two parties are pinnacles of pyramids, a heightening of observable characteristics. As a coalition Labour is more an illustration of the components. The Parliamentary Labour Party embodies a

contradiction deep in the heart of Labour; it is both a crusade
– what the French call a *partie du mouvement* – and an insti-
tution – an incumbent party in what has been a two-party system in the five decades since the great depression congealed
party differences into two. It is a parliamentary party
working the system but part of a broad 'labour movement'
outside. Labour must be both. As such it is inevitably schizo-
phrenic. The crusade is the drive but incumbency confers the
possibility of power without which the ambitions cannot be
realised. It also imposes constraints and responsibilities
which conflict with the natural restlessness of movement.
Winning power requires dilution of pristine objectives and
brings disappointment for the enthusiast. The attitudes and
aspirations of men anxious to run an old earth are very different from the more passionate concerns of those keen to build
a new heaven. Labour is in a state of permanent, built-in tension between government men, the ministrables, minds
focussed on power, and the opposition mentality pre-
occupied with policy, progress and perfection. To enthuse
supporters it has to dress and behave in one fashion. To
achieve, it needs another. Crusade is a matter of narrow,
boring commitment. Politics is a question of broad appeals to
the lowest common denominator.

This tension characterised the Liberal government of
1906–14, when they were the party of change, and the great
1945–51 Labour government, architect of the welfare state.
It is found in every other socialist party and in the American
Democratic Party. What distinguishes the others from Britain's Labour Party is the fact that here the schizophrenia is
built into the organisation: the Labour leader has to play
simultaneously in two theatres to two audiences. Tension
hardly mattered when there was pride in winning, in taking
the people to power, in achieving. As that was taken for
granted the audience in the other theatre became more critical. A din of dissent moved from a background rumble into
a continuing roar. It did so because Labour has been less successful. Success is not measured in electoral terms, for on this
score Labour has done moderately well: more years in power
since the war than Australian or New Zealand Labour
Parties, less than the Scandinavian; more successful than the

southern European parties, less than the northern. The crucial test is that power had brought disappointment. The 1945–51 government had built the world's first welfare state. Yet the Wilson government of 1964–70 had disappointed economically. Despite a huge majority, it had not delivered the satisfaction, the rising standard of living, the improving conditions, the better public services that the electorate was coming to expect as of right.

The failure was Britain's. She was growing faster than ever before and yet more slowly than any of the advanced industrial countries. Elsewhere, post-war capitalism had discovered the secret of exponential growth in full employment and a rich mass consumer market providing a high and growing demand. High investment and expanding world trade allowed an export-led growth which in turn produced more investment, more productivity and hence more growth. Economists labelled this the German miracle or the Japanese miracle, not noticing that it was also the French miracle, the Swedish miracle and practically everyone's but Britain's. Britain lagged partly because she devoted more to consumption, the result of pleasing electorates, and so investing less, but the main explanation was a simple truism: she did not grow because she did not grow. No government paid the same continuous attention to building up and strengthening industry and production that competitors did. Production was treated as a given, something inevitable and needing no encouragement. The interests of the financial community were dominant over those of production and everything else. The economy was managed by interest rates and as each burst of expansion sucked in imports and threatened the balance of payments and hence the pound, it was dampened down by deflation and higher interest rates, thus penalising anyone who had gone for growth or invested, rewarding those who played safe and thought small. So began stop-go. The stops got deeper, the goes shorter and more whimpering, bringing Britain to comparative decline against more rapidly growing economies elsewhere, and imposing similar deflationary strategies on both parties in power.

Britain's parties were less successful because her economy was. Their responses were different. Conservatives cast around for new ways to make things work: modernisation, Common Market, Selsdon deflation, expansion, then the Monetarism, which was essentially a counter-revolution against 1945 carried through by a small town Poujadist brought up to scrimping, saving and the politics of the *Daily Express*, the *Daily Mail* and Hayek under the bed-clothes. Labour persevered with its old policies, attempting to keep a rickety machine going, but its supporters cast around for explanations: not enough socialism, or too much, the trade union tie, the failure to develop new policies beyond a revisionism which had been orthodoxy ever since Crosland wrote *The Future of Socialism* in 1956. All these explanations were proferred for a failure which would not have been felt had Labour been as successful in office as the German SPD or the Scandinavian Social Democratic Parties. The difference was not that they disavowed Marxism or that British Labour was more old-fashioned but that they presided over expanding, growing economies. Britain's share of world trade was falling steadily and the nation was in comparative decline.

The latent tension within the party, instead of being diluted by success, was compounded by comparative failure. The left, the oppositionists, would still have argued for more socialism, purer principle, but the demand would have been less credible, and less likely to be heard against a government which pointed to prosperity and whose successes would almost certainly have been endorsed by a grateful electorate as they were elsewhere. Instead comparative decline ushered in the years of instability. Electors cast around for hope and cast out governments as they failed. Social democratic revisionism, though it remained the orthodoxy, was not seen to work. Untried and probably untriable alternatives were far more attractive. The test in politics is neither principle nor purity but success. Its measurement is votes. Labour had failed by 1970.

The failure was not yet crucial. The internal opposition were noisy but the leadership was still respected. Things would be better next time. The social democratic orthodoxy was challenged by a new fundamentalism, by Marxism, by those who wanted to go further faster or to strengthen the role of the state by imposing planning agreements on firms and by taking more control and greater power to direct investment and plan the economy. Yet it was always possible to argue, and certainly true, that the problem was not one of the degree of socialism but competence; Labour governments had not concentrated on production and investment. If they had done so growth would have been forthcoming, given firmer priorities and greater clear-headedness next time. Exaggerated out of all proportion by a media ever anxious to heighten division in Labour's ranks, the paper tiger of the new left was routinely beaten off by Harold Wilson. He declined to accept commitments to nationalise a specified number of companies, diluted planning agreements, isolated Tony Benn and then transferred him to the Siberian Power Station of Energy. 'We are the Masters still,' the revisionists might have said.

In 1974 they faced their second chance. Unlike cats, they could not expect nine lives but the chance was taken up in the worst possible circumstances for the situation in which they took power compelled them not to expand but to protect, not to rebuild but to save from collapse. The oil crisis discredited Edward Heath's policies and brought him into confrontation with the miners. Labour came in to save the situation and clean up the Tory mess, a traditional role but one to be accomplished in the face of galloping inflation and with no majority. Labour had not won the 1974 election. It had just been better at not losing than the Tories. Support for both parties fell. Heath's fell faster than Wilson's who was left holding the crisis.

The 1974–79 government became not a testing ground for the social democratic reform but a holding operation, keeping a rickety economy going by elastic bands, pieces of string and bits of sealing wax. On objective grounds this Wilson–Callaghan government was a comparative success. Facing the backwash of the collapse of the Heath expansion programme and the impact of the first great oil crisis, a government with no majority restored control by an incomes policy which brought inflation down from astronomic figures to below 10 per cent. It kept public spending up to protect the needy, improve welfare and keep economic activity as high as was possible at a time when the dynamics of the economy were faltering. It protected the people by supporting threatened jobs, developing schemes to provide substitutes, cushioning unemployment and the standards of those unable to look after themselves. This was a policy of equality of sacrifice, not relaunch. Yet it brought the country through. Achieved in the face of the most serious economic difficulties since the war, and sustained with a vanishing majority which, after 1977, was gone altogether, it constituted success. Britain's inflation rate, initially outstripping industrial competitors, was down to the OECD average by 1979. The unemployment rate, increasing with the imposed deflation of 1976, was then lower than the average. Investment was pushed up to a higher level than ever before. After its painful adjustment, Britain managed both growth and falling unemployment. She had come through. Not well, but adequately.

Practicality did not mean acceptance. The left built up an impressive charge sheet: the failure to make planning agreements compulsory, incomes policy, cuts in government spending, the pact with the Liberals in 1977. It was also extending its control over the National Executive Committee. The twelve trade union representatives remained on balance amenable to the leadership but less so the women's section and the constituencies, becoming a base for the frustrated left in the PLP – Allaun, Benn, Heffer, Kinnock, Joan Lestor, Jo Richardson and the political thinker Dennis Skinner. Their leadership changed it from a nagging handmaiden to public opposition, constantly criticising the government and developing its own policies, published in 1976 as *Labour's Programme*, a radical amalgam very different from what the government was actually doing.

It was difficult to argue that more determined socialism would have strengthened prospects of survival. Muttering darkly, the left had to go along with government policies. They raised all too little protest at the real failure of the government, the refusal from 1977 to opt for the genuine new initiative which then became possible by going for growth and expansion through lower interest rates and a competitive exchange rate designed to give the export-led growth for which the IMF had intended its 1976 measures to pave the way. Instead the government, its nerve broken by the collapse of the pound in 1976, feeling itself dependent on the goodwill of the IMF and the 'confidence' of an increasingly orthodox financial community at home, went out of its way to display its own orthodoxy. It introduced the monetarist trojan horse by proclaiming M3 targets for money supply. To keep them it allowed the pound to rise as the oil began to come on stream, thus nipping in the bud the recovery begun in 1977, bringing in imports to weaken domestic production (but help to hold down inflation) and keeping interest rates high. A great opportunity was lost. Monetarism was introduced and house-trained by Labour, ready for the Conservatives to turn it into the only instrument of policy with disastrous effects on the prospects for growth.

Labour's left, always more concerned about ideology than economic practicality, was curiously silent on this major abdication. The left saw its role as the voice of principle, a voice which came through clearest when it spoke in unison with the trade unions. Through the abdications and equivocations of the Wilson years it had wavered because the trade unions had backed the government up to 1969 and *In Place of Strife*. When they cooled overnight the left became stronger because the unions were more sympathetic. Sympathy faded with the Social Contract. When Labour came back to power, the unions supported it and developed their own incomes policy to save it. That support got cooler as the government kept incomes policy longer than the unions had intended. They found it irksome but were prepared to accept it, though not forever. The real blow came with Jim Callaghan's decision not to call the election in October 1978. The unions had expected it and tolerated incomes policy on that understanding. The polls indicated that Labour was likely to get back, certainly as the largest single party, if not with an overall majority. The 1978 Trades Union Conference was intended as a pre-election rally for the Callaghan government but Jim decided to go his own way. Encouraged by Michael Foot, strongly supported by David Owen and Merlyn Rees, who considered that the minor parties could be managed, he opted to carry on into 1979 and hope for better things. Without consulting the unions or even forewarning them, he went down to the TUC conference at Brighton and told the world he was soldiering on.

Jim Callaghan was a consummate political manager, a master of the House of Commons and of the moods of his party, always right on his short-term calculations, always wrong on the major issues. As Moses, he would have mistimed his arrival at the parting of the waters. He did so now and got instead the water workers' strike. The organisation of the trade unions and the loyalty of their members had been disastrously strained by the prolongation of incomes policy. Now, insult was added to injury by tightening it. With inflation running at 8 per cent, the government decided to go for broke. The original White Paper proposal for an 8 per cent pay policy was deleted the day before publication and 5 per cent substituted, a gesture of confidence but largely at the expense of the unions. Bluff became desperate when the only backing for the policy, sanctions against private firms, was knocked out by a vote in the House of Commons in December. Tories who wanted no incomes policy united with the Liberals who wanted a stronger one and a few Labour rebels who wanted clear consciences. The government had been skating on thin ice for so long that it hardly noticed that there was now no ice at all. Next year came the disaster; the drivers' strike, the Ford strike, both for higher pay, the health service and dirty jobs strike against low pay. Those who had most to lose and those who had most to gain from incomes policy struck against it. It collapsed. With it went the relationship between government and the unions and the remaining credibility of the administration. The public had not been enthusiastic about Labour but had given it high marks for getting and keeping the cooperation of the trade unions in contrast to the Tories. That cooperation was shattered and the 1978–79 winter of discontent ruined the government. For the public it was a simple practical test. Labour had failed. For the left in the Labour Party it was a vindication: government failed because it had defied conference decisions against incomes policy. The unions were alienated, less ready to back a leadership they no longer trusted against a left which, on that issue at least, had been on their side.

The backwash of disappointment and defeat was the fertile soil in which the dragon's teeth were planted. To it were added other rich fertilisers: class antagonism towards the smooth men of power; a feeling of distance from a PLP which was inevitably remote because the Commons were; the restless frustrations of the activist. All these were constants. The real reason for success was the reaction against the Callaghan government.

The collapse of that government reversed the balance of power in the party. The left and the national executive had been increasingly strident but Jim Callaghan had always been able to put issues to the basic test of loyalty: did they want the government to carry on or to replace it by a Tory administration whose propensities were becoming increasingly ominous? This last restraint, the ultimate dog lead, was now gone. The leadership had failed and was discredited. The unions and the party had been put under the maximum strain to support a government which had collapsed. The result of the strain was that both became far more difficult to control just when the leadership had less authority to control them. The demise of every Labour government has seen a revival of the left, demands for more radical policies. That now became resurgence. The left was already dominant in conference and controlling the national executive by seventeen left to twelve centre right (11–1 in constituency and women's sections 3–9 in the trade unions). The defeat of the government meant not only the triumph of Margaret Thatcher but of the internal opposition within the Labour Party. Both said that the Callaghan failure was not to be repeated.

What was discredited in 1979 was two decades of Labour Party politics. Revisionism, predicated on increasing public spending based on growth, had run into the problem that growth had not been forthcoming. So the public spending had to be financed out of taxation and had generated anger and discontent. With it was weakened, to the point of being undermined, the party leadership of the Callaghans and the Wilsons, a generation of senior figures identified with the governments of the 1960s and 1970s, the preeminence of the parliamentary party and the old tolerant compromises to preserve a bickering unity. The cooperation between the official leadership of the trade unions and Labour leaders was also a casualty. The trade unions had seen their internal cohesion undermined, their leaderships weakened and power transferred from the centre to the shop floor. The party had dwindled in numbers to the point where it was now dominated by unrepresentative activists and much more middle class, one study showing 57 per cent of conference delegates to be middle class, 60 per cent public sector employees with the YAP professions, the talkers, becoming increasingly dominant and driving others away as they did so.

In the new situation of more acute economic difficulties, some said capitalist collapse, the ameliorative approach, making capitalism better, appeared outdated and irrelevant. New, harder doctrines came to the fore. In the 1950s political scientists talked of the death of ideology. Now the hearse seemed to be waiting for pragmatism. It had meant slow progress. Born-again ideology promised faster. Industrial muscle and shopfloor power were increasing pressure on the slow-growing economy's ability to deliver. On the intellectual shopfloor pressure groups and campaigns, the picket lines and the demonstrations, showed the same urgency. The pace was quickening on the left, as Labour's slowed. Yet there was also a whole new culture, an end to submissiveness and deference, a greater willingness to question, argue and dispute. The old days of 'children should be seen and not heard' lingered on in the attitudes of an older generation of leaders surprised at the lack of respect, the constant need to justify. It was gone among younger followers and among an electorate which knew its politicians, their strengths and weaknesses, through television and had more information and facts to throw at them.

The whole atmosphere became more negative, particularly in the Labour Party and towards MPs. The cult of youth, the cultural phenomenon of the 1960s, reached the Labour Party a decade later. Its adherents were then middle-aged yet appeared young to an aging party led by Jim Callaghan, Michael Foot and Denis Healey. There was a total gulf of mood and attitudes between the generations. Pragmatism and patience were countered by ideology and anger. The pop-Marxism of 1968 had simply transferred from instant revolution to the short jog through the Labour Party. Ideology sanctioned naivety, impetuousity and abandonment of the hard-learned lessons of party operation through the decades. Capitalism was collapsing so the pace could be accelerated. Gradualism was now outdated and so were all the compromises that went with it. The older generation was hesitant and equivocal, the younger had all the confidence of this half-baked ideology. It was also articulate, the products of the post-war educational revolution, the polyocracy to Alan Watkins, the polytrotracy to others, not rounded or even 'educated' but able to defend its instincts by ideology in a way the older generation had never been able to do. Socially they were now educated working class in middle-class jobs. But not very good ones. They spoke in the name of the working class, even in its accent, but not with its consent, for its interests were different, more practical, less ideological. In the view of the new left the proletariat had moved away from Labour because it had deserted socialism. A return to socialist basics, combined with the increasing pressures of the collapse of capitalism, would bring revival of proletarian consciousness as a new and more powerful dynamic for the party, as soon as all the compromises, betrayals and mistakes of appealing to the centre were sloughed off. Unfortunately a lot of babies were thrown out with some very murky bath water.

There was left not one but a whole range of groups and opinions. The real distinction between it and the left of the 1950s and 1960s was different conditioning, the fact that Marx was making a bigger impact than at any time since the 1930s, and that the left was now preponderant and better organised but still opposition-minded. The reaction against the leadership and the long dominance of the right had given it sufficient unity and strength to carry all before it, but insufficient responsibility to calculate what came next when it did. The old alumni association of the left was the Tribune group, bigger than ever at seventy-strong but looking increasingly old-fashioned, even tamed by the parliamentary club. They had kept the torch of 'socialism' alive by constantly asking for more public spending, nationalisation, nuclear disarmament: the politics of Oliver Twist. They had been prepared to vote against the Callaghan government, whenever its existence was not in danger. Yet Michael Foot was in the cabinet, they were divided on incomes policy and on the Common Market where the 1975 referendum had in any case concreted the issue over. So Tribunites offered not an ideology but a left sentimentalism, attached to the slogans of the left, responding to its conditioned reflexes, angry at any threat to its sacred cows. They needed the leadership to react against. As a force, Tribune was house-trained and entirely predictable, a shoal to navigate round but one which presented no danger of shipwreck.

The old left were the insiders. The new left were outsiders stronger in the constituencies and particularly the cities, gaining ground rapidly in London, looking to the party and conference rather than parliament. The old 'left' welcomed the new left as reinforcements in the good old cause, an infusion of youth into an aging clique, another group who talked the same language, or at least responded to the same slogans. Trojans welcomed the horse in the same way. The new left were in fact a very different breed; younger, more ideological, more Marxist and above all, more organised, a contrast between the Old Contemptibles and the SAS.

The right was entrenched in the parliamentary party, dominating its elections, conditioning its thinking. Yet the parliamentary party had exhausted itself, and its credit, in the struggle to keep the Callaghan government going through the years of the vanishing majority. This absorption had pulled it away from the party outside, for the parliamentary struggle took precedence. When the Callaghan government collapsed, the discredit and disappointment weakened the Parliamentary Labour Party which had been its prop. When Labour governments lose, power shifts to the outside party and the focus passes away from the parliamentary party in its backwater to the outside organisation. That natural development was now heightened by the discredit and disappointment.

The left had better bases, not for reaching the public, but for carrying on the argument in the party. It had become increasingly powerful in the constituencies. The Peter Walker reorganisation of local government reduced the numbers of councillors and deprived constituency Labour parties of the ballast of experience and moderation. The decline in numbers of party members went on through the Callaghan years, just as it had done before, and was compounded by the hefty increase in subscriptions: £1.20 in 1979, £5 by 1981, £6 in 1982. All this made the left stronger because less diluted, as well as less representative of the Labour vote for, with an average Labour vote of 20,000 per constituency in 1979, the average membership was only 2 per cent of it and the average GMC only fifty strong. The old working-class membership drifted away; new, better-educated, more articulate and more middle-class groups, many of them from the public sector, came in, making the departures worse because the older generation often felt inadequate at dealing with them. The party of the skilled workers and the improving working class was becoming the party of the improved, and particularly those in the public sector. An instrument of advancement was becoming one for protecting an entrenched vested interest.

Constituency parties, particularly those without a Labour MP to act as a link with reality, were first disappointed, then hostile to the Wilson–Callaghan administrations, a hostility expressed in their conference resolutions and by their delegates. Conference was less and less manageable, the NEC an institutionalised opposition to the government, keeping up a barracking hostility. Callaghan could often get his way, yet increasingly he had to do it by bluff, by ignoring conference, as in 1978 when it came out against incomes policy, or by *force majeure*. He drew up the 1979 election manifesto at short notice, using the cabinet majority to reject, emasculate or water down most of the proposals the NEC put up. The myth of the great betrayal gained currency though it was as much due to frequency of repetitions as accuracy. To talk of 'the left' is media-speak, a necessary shorthand but a distortion. The left comes in fifty-seven varieties. Three categories will explain. The old 'Tribune' left was the parliamentary kop, the focus of a discontent directed against power and orthodoxy. The left elected to Parliament has no alternative but to join it and constituency parties have made others. Yet it is irrelevant to the real left. This subdivides, the sectarian left on the wilder shores of Labour and outside it and the 'hard' left inside the party. Both share common characteristics and peculiarities. As George Orwell put it, ' . . . the mere words "Socialism" and "Communism" draw towards themselves with magnetic force every fruit-juice drinker, nudist, sandal-wearer, sex-maniac, Quaker, "Nature cure" quack, pacifist and feminist in England.' Green movements and green politics, and he could have added Marxist, Trotskyist, Buddhist, Trotskyoid and Marxoid, all recognisable by the jargon, the emphasis on 'struggle' and capitalist collapse, a belief which inevitably discounts the slow plodding methods of politics by providing short-cuts. Marxism has always played a part, albeit small, in the British Labour movement. Many of the new men were different, for Marxist-Leninism was their ideology, a different and far more dangerous body of thought, embracing the vanguard party and the dictatorship of the proletariat, and so totally alien to Labour's approach. Trotsky was there, too, to play his old nuisance role of unreasonable demands to generate alienation, an ideological excuse for a destabilisation worthy of CIA financing.

The other common pattern was clamorous divisiveness. They had no loyalty to a Labour Party they were using. Trotsky said the Labour Party and the trade unions

> are the main prop of British imperialism and of the European, if not the world, bourgeoisie. Workers must at all costs be shown those self-satisfied pedants, drivelling eclectics, sentimental careerists and liveried footmen of the bourgeoisie in their true colours, to show them up for what they are means to discredit them beyond repair.*

For the party their arrival and increasing influence was all loss. Labour either accepted them and suffered the consequent discredit, as well as the nuisance of having its discussions and decisions hijacked into areas irrelevant to real life, or it attempted to exclude and control them, enraging lunatics all over the country unable to see the difference between

* L. Trotsky, *Where is Britain Going?*, 1925, p. 58.

giving a home to parasites and free speech. For the arrivals themselves it was an all-win situation. Either they rode on Labour's back to power and opened up horizons unthinkable to others of their sectarian disposition or they weakened and discredited the party and proved all that they said and believed about it as an unsuitable vehicle for socialism.

The sectarian left is characterised by the continuous creation of groupings. 'Wherever there is an idiocy unvoiced a left group will step into the vacuum.'* All compete to be more Trotsky than thou but since they blossom and die or break up like amoebae any listing is more a seed catalogue than a firm offer. The Proscribed List originally drew a line between them and the Labour Party. This was abolished in a fit of democratic enthusiasm, so the remaining distinction is whether or not they have the money, and pigheaded obstinacy, to put candidates up against Labour. Those who did not were free to come into the party. Tiring of the futility of sectarian life, many did, introducing as they did so the same attitudes and preoccupations into their new home. Labour in some areas became the people's dispensary for sick Trotskyites.

Ignoring such antediluvian creatures as the Communist Party, New Communists, CP of GB (Marxist-Leninist) and the Revolutionary Communists, the main fringe groups are:

Militant
A party within the party but disguised as a periodical, its NEC the editorial board, its branches, the readers' meetings, its ideology ESN Trotskyism distilled in a paper, each issue of which is the same and in speeches reduced to the recycling of jargon. With a continuous existence running from Ted Grant and a group of South African Trots emerging into a later vintage from the University of Sussex, descending through the Revolutionary Socialist League to the movement of today, *Militant* is more of a museum piece than a threat, the old subverting the young by taking them out of the real world and having the same relation to real politics as Moonies to religion. Yet Militant has sixty-six full time workers,

---

* Prunelle Kaur, *Go Forth and Multiply*, 1983, p. 26.

thirty-four of them in the provinces, and effectively domi-
nates the Labour Party Young Socialists, who are reduced to
selling *Militant* to each other, their meetings interchangeable
with Militant's. Which is the reason why they never have
above 10,000 members at any time when one young person
in two can't get a job.

Socialist Workers Party

'The smallest mass party in the world.' More open to trends
and fads than *Militant*, it is smaller, its *Socialist Worker* has
a much lower circulation because it centres around one man,
Tony Cliffe, not the team and guru approach *Militant*
prefers.

International Marxist Group

Once, with Robin Blackburn, the matinee idols of Trotskyism, now aging and split, half determined to 'dissolve into
Labour Party' though a few solids like Tariq Ali, who left
them in 1981, have been stopped in the Hornsea treatment
works; half happy to change names to the Socialist league
and carry on Trotskyism as usual.

The Workers Revolutionary Party

Show-biz politics with Vanessa Redgrave and the actor–pro-
ducer Gerry Healey, another dinosaur of Trotskyism and the
pioneer of Militant-style infiltration into the Socialist Labour
League which penetrated and took over the Young Socialists
in the early 1960s pioneering *Militant*'s later takeover.
Because those were less tolerant times it was expelled for its
pains in 1965 with the disbanding of some local parties at the
same time. This is now the only group with a daily paper,
Newsline, full colour and no readership. Where its money
comes from is easy to guess but difficult to state. The same
money finances writs on the same generous scale.

The Chartists

Characterised by a determination to make Labour a revolutionary party and a belief in catastrophism. The final crisis is
near, though it does keep having to be postponed.

The ILP
Longest standing loony left, so old it was breeding its own
members until the 1970s when it was infiltrated, changed its
name from Independent Labour 'Party' to 'Publications' and
became a pressure group within the party, first on the left of
the left and now on the right of the left.

London Labour Briefing
The Horatio Bottomley of Trotskyism. A monthly opinion
sheet, 30p, funded by the London Labour Party and run by
an editorial collective with no line except abuse of the right
and tolerance of every loony view, particularly sexy ones; the
intellectual equivalent of the *Sun*.

The Socialist Campaign for a Labour Victory
Formed in 1978 and similar to *Militant* but more trendy and
feminist. Publishes the weekly *Socialist Organiser* and in
open dispute with *Militant* in many Labour branches in
places such as Oxford, where Alan Thornett's Workers
Socialist League merged with it, one of the few known Trot
fusions.

Because the frontier guard on the Labour Party has been
abolished, such groups and their members can wander in and
out of the party. Their impact has been enormously exaggerated by a press campaign to portray their efforts as communist infiltration. The operation is in fact play-school
Marxism, a nuisance and an embarrassment, not a take-over.
Yet it can build up a fluctuating strength in decayed urban
parties, by concentrating bed-sit brigades in key places. The
organisation is 'available' and in the case of *Militant* it is
thrown into any left-wing campaign running. The 'incumbents' brought a new tone of hostility to established leadership, discredited the party in the eyes of the public and
reinforced sectarianism. Labour suddenly found itself pre-
occupied with common basics which should have been taken
for granted: time spent endlessly explaining why the nationalisation of 250 monopolies is not immediately possible is not
time well spent.
   The real problem was one usually confused with this fringe

left organisation within the party. In the past this had worked from the top down. Now it was bottom up, extra-parliamentary and far more powerful. Most effective was the open conspiracy of the Campaign for Labour Party Democracy. This had wide-ranging support in the party because it confined itself strictly to the aim of democracy. It backed this by the new techniques of organising groups in constituencies all over the country, by circulating model resolutions to be sent to Conference and NEC and by developing common strategies. Thus it introduced a new element into Labour's shambling and infinitely exploitable structure, a tight, disciplined organisation dedicated to limited objectives. Its ideological counterpart was the Labour Coordinating Committee, a policy pressure group organised from the top downwards to provide a platform and extra-parliamentary organisation for the new left as *Tribune* had never done for the old. The umbrella organisation bringing all the left groups together was the Rank and File Mobilising Committee, set up in 1979 to coordinate the activities of groups including *Militant* and the Labour Party Young Socialists which it had largely taken over. The techniques of the CLPD were being exploited by the entire new left for their common purposes. The testing ground was London where the left was stronger, more prepared to shunt an old leadership aside and able to embark on its techniques of purifying the party by rigorous selection of GLC candidates and unremitting concentration on the development of a radical manifesto as the centre of strategy. The GLC was to be the test bed for the New Model Labour Party.

The new left appeared more formidable than it was. Its organisation was effective largely because there was nothing to counter it. Its ideology appeared clearer because of concentration on limited objectives. The participants appeared more dominant because the right, the leadership and the parliamentary party were discredited and disorientated. Given time, all these weaknesses would have become clear, the gaps between the old left and the new would have widened, the fissiparous nature of the new Marxism would have gone its inevitable way and the differences of viewpoint and objective would have become more apparent. Given time trade union leaderships, as much threatened as the party, would have

asserted themselves and organised to beat off the threat
while the right would have organised its own counter-action.

Time was not available. The left campaign was not slow to
build up as in the past. It was already running at full strength,
controlling major positions of power, when the government
was defeated. The collapse of leadership authority created a
vacuum. The new campaign stepped immediately into it.
More important it also had a leader, a *deus ex machina*, even
if the *machina* he was ex was the Callaghan government
itself. Aneurin Bevan had taken time to constitute himself a
leader of the internal opposition in the 1950s. Even then his
flawed genius had made him a maverick major. Michael Foot
had never asserted himself. Now Tony Benn was ready. He
became the figure around whom all the disparate parts of an
inherently disunited movement could rally. His prestige
strengthened them. He could confirm their worst fears of
betrayal and treachery at the top, saying, 'You are right. It
is so. They will betray. I can show you that they did.'

As the eminence, increasingly *grise*, of the new movement,
Tony Benn is an enigma. Presented as the philosopher of the
new socialism, he had none of the stigmata of the intellectual, and his doctrines were drawn more from old-fashioned
radicalism than socialism. The main badge of the intellectual
was the long record of changes of mind, a progress which the
uncharitable saw as opportunism. A revisionist supporter of
Gaitskell in the 1950s, he was easily hurt because the leader
had not paid enough attention to him. By 1963 he was an
energetic advocate of the public relations politics of
Kennedyism, a dynamic hundred days of action irrespective
of substance. As the guru of technology, he preached it
almost as a new religion. From the 1970 defeat he had moved
left, flirting with Marxism though never consummating the
relationship, venerating the working class, its traditions and
institutions and particularly the trade unions, as only
someone from a genuine upper-class background can.
Whether the motive was ambition, incompetently pursued,
or a propensity to take intellectual enthusiasm to absurd conclusions, was never clear. What was clear was that the man
aroused strong antagonism. Erstwhile colleagues saw one of
themselves whipping up hostility to a Labour government of

which he had been such a senior figure with anger amounting to hysteria. He was exploiting the common discredit for his own purposes. They had all toiled in the vineyards to produce the sour wine and got no credit. Tony Benn toasted in it, exempted from all the criticism of every Labour government of which he had been a part, and received an adulation they richly envied. He told his supporters:

> We have seen twenty years of surrender. Since 1959 the parliamentary leadership of the Labour Party has been going along with the idea that the post-war consensus built upon full employment and the welfare state was a permanent feature of life in Britain and that trade unionism would be brought into a position where it helped to run it. That response has failed to command the support of our people because they have seen first that it did not contain within it any element whatsoever of transformation and second that even by its own criteria it failed. That policy could not bring about growth and could not extend freedom.*

His Marxism showed itself in the belief that capitalism was collapsing:

> We are locked into a virtual collapse of our industry which has proceeded more rapidly than people expected and which has been coming for some time. This decline is beginning at a lower level of activity than we had in the 1930s and forms part of a world capitalist crisis which at the moment is also deepening with very severe unemployment in the United States and in the EEC.†

Everywhere among those tinged with Marxism this was a common belief which sanctioned new types of policy and behaviour. Yet Tony Benn's deductions from it were differ-

* T. Benn and E. Hobsbawn, *The Forward March of Labour Halted*, 1981, p. 78.
† Ibid., p. 75.

ent. Where others put the emphasis on economic strategies advocating policies which might not otherwise have been acceptable but were now sanctioned by inevitability, he looked to old-fashioned ultra-democracy:

> There are in fact a number of parallel crises in train at the same time and that is why I think we have to look at them not only in terms of socialist analysis but also in terms of a direct sustained socialist challenge everywhere in the world to the secretive exercise of centralised power working through bureaucracy . . . The particular characteristic of the British corporate state is that in this country mediaeval feudalism has lasted so long that it has fused with modern corporatism and created a most astonishing centralised block of political, financial and industrial power which has now virtually succeeded in defeating Parliament as an effective countervailing force, defeating Labour's rank and file and commanding the general support of the civil service and the mass media. That is an authoritarian system.*

Economic decline could be dealt with by the Alternative Economic Strategy, a *dirigiste* structure of state management of the economy, import controls and greater state control, which had emerged in the 1970s from the efforts of the Cambridge Economic Policy Group to make the economy fit for Keynes to live in and the predispositions of Marxist economists. The real problem was power, a structure of control so overwhelming it was going to be difficult to make headway against. Yet Tony Benn himself was an optimist. His commitment to democracy was as passionate and as mystical as his commitment to technology had been in the 1960s. It was selective, attacking private monoliths not unions, encouraging activists, not, now, referenda, eschewing representative democracy. Yet it was passionate and that was enough to carry it through illogicalities and impracticability. Benn became at once the natural, inevitable, and only, leader of the resurgent left. In combination he and they posed a bigger

* Ibid., pp. 77 and 99.

threat than either separately. The leader gave them a focus and a credibility. They gave him an enthusiastic backing. They were more powerful than any opposition had ever been within the Labour Party and operated in an aging, rheumatic party whose membership was falling, whose leadership was exhausted from the struggle for survival, whose credit was running out, not only with the electorate but with its own people.

> The questions of policy have been argued out in great detail since the 1972 conference. I don't say that conference policy is perfect because it clearly isn't but it offers a reasonably consistent and different view . . . That view now has a majority position. So I suppose the biggest difference between the position in which I find myself now, as compared to 1951 when Aneurin resigned, was that he was then a minority and minorities – especially left minorities – can face great difficulties within the party. Now of course, partly because the left couldn't get a majority, a lot of people who should now be in the Labour Party disappeared into community groups, into ultra-left movements and so on. Now that the Labour Party has got a majority around alternative – and Socialist – policies you are going to find that many of these people who left us in the sixties will be rejoining us. And that is going to consolidate that majority.*

Labour was to be transformed.

---

* Ibid., p. 87.

3 · Launching the Red Titanic

The organic sickness of British capitalism means the inevitability of new splits in the Labour Party. That section of the right wing which calculated that the best interests of their 'careers' stood in remaining within the Labour Party and holding it firmly and organically linked to the umbilical cord of capitalism will find the ground more and more disappearing from under their feet. Both before and after the next general election there can be a process of desertion to the Social Democrats.

MILITANT

The proudest claim of the left has always been to be the conscience of the party. The voice is neither still nor small, for high principle is often taken to require equal volume, but it speaks for purity and progress, a constant reminder to Labour governments conditioned by the compromises of power of the bedrock of principle on which the party rests. The left, therefore, has an oppositionist role. Usually it finds itself in conflict with a leadership of which it is congenitally suspicious. It also has a policy role, always preoccupied with the issues, those of ideology such as nationalisation and government spending and even more those of foreign policy on which conscience is best aired in such problems as colonialism and the third world or the cold wars in the 1940s, nuclear weapons and German rearmament in the 1950s, Vietnam in the 1960s, the arms race and the new cold war in the 1970s. On all these issues the voice of conscience became particularly shrill.

The new left was different. The various lefts of the past had been concerned with ideas, convinced that argument and persuasion would eventually triumph. Now cynicism was driving out optimism. Where Michael Foot and Bevan had seen parliament as the great platform for ideas in a debate about hearts and minds, the new left had little respect for the talking shop and questioned its value. Nor were they inclined to trust Labour leaders. To lead was to betray. Leadership itself was an antisocial act, an indictable offence. Leaders would sell out – unless they were stopped. This argument was not about principle but power. Policy took second place, partly because views were taken for granted, almost common ground among all right-, or rather left-, thinking folk. If they weren't such there was even more reason to ignore them because differences would lead to antagonism and division among the left. Far better than sullying principles with practicalities was common zeal and decisive action in the workers' struggle.

The real problem with policies was not so much what they were as to get them implemented. That required a total change in the power structure of the party to transform it from a loose coalition, with broad common denominator principles responding to leadership, into a more coherent, tightly disciplined, party united on a common set of policies and structured so as to be able to force those policies through by discipline. The pattern was not dissimilar to continental Marxist parties but their discipline was centralised, enforced by the centre party and running from the top down. Such democratic centralism in a British context would have entrenched a Callaghan leadership which the left had come to regard as another form of Stalinism. Here the power base was to be the activist, whether in the constituencies or in the trade unions, where power was slipping away from the old boss machines of the 1950s to the liberated shop floor.

This was not democracy. Activists themselves are an elite, distinguished by attitudes, intellectualism, public service jobs and educational background, and indeed by activity itself, for political involvement is not a sign of normality. So different were they that they almost assumed a vanguard role, empowered to speak for the masses, not because they represented them, but because they understood the ideological trends of the times, the direction of history. All this meant fragmentation of power at the top and required control from the bottom up, in clear distinction to both Labour's old easy-going leadership and the media-generated star system which some called presidential politics, others leader appeal. It fitted uneasily into a parliamentary tradition which the party had always espoused for its leadership nucleus. The PLP had a dual responsibility to both party and to constituents which was difficult to reconcile to the tighter framework of control now being advocated. The member of parliament had always regarded himself as a representative. He was being asked to assume a role more akin to that of delegate, a change in the terms and conditions of his employment as well as in the whole nature of the system.

The difference was partly one of perspective. Labour attitudes had been formed in the long period of opposition, the slow pre-war rise to majority status, the abrupt fall of 1951, then the long struggle to get back through the affluent 1950s. The central preoccupation was thus the difficulties of achieving office, the need to win support, please the people, build up a majority and dilute the purity of pristine principle. New left attitudes were formed in a period when Labour looked more like the inevitable incumbent, the Wilson years of the 1960s, the 1974–79 government brought in to clear up the mess left by a Tory government which appeared too incompetent to rule. At the very least the 'in out' changes of the 1960s and 1970s seemed to guarantee that Labour and Tory would alternate in power. Thus power was taken for granted, the real problem was what to do with it – how to prevent the politics of Tweedle Dum and Tweedle Dee – how to keep principle clear. Some assumed that Labour would come to power as Tory governments inevitably failed and built up a backwash of popularity as both Alec Douglas Home and Ted Heath had done and Margaret Thatcher, because more stupid and politically prejudiced than either, must surely do more quickly. The majority, more ideologically motivated, were even more confident. Labour would come to power because capitalism was collapsing. The best means of getting there was to revive the political consciences of a proletariat disillusioned by the enforced diet of betrayals Labour governments had enforced on them. As the new left authors of *Manifesto* put it,

Labour lost much of its traditional support because part of the movement, especially its official representatives and leaders, abandoned a class-based socialist strategy in favour of a compromise with the existing structure of power. Revisionism or, as it came to be known, social democracy, deprived Labour of a coherent analysis, drastically weakened its political programme and undermined the credibility of the socialist values and the party itself. A second fundamental cause of Labour's loss of support has been the manner in which Labour MPs, ministers and trade union leaders exercised political and industrial power. In their dealings with top management in parliament and in government, Labour leaders adopted the style of the ruling class . . . Already many who perceive themselves to be excluded from power are beginning to bring a new vitality to the Labour movement. Shop stewards, council tenants, pensioners, teachers, workers in the public services and now also women and ethnic minorities have started to see the Labour Party as a possible vehicle for advancing their causes in a common movement.*

A curious mixture of the sociology of a pluralist society and a Marxism harking back to a more monolithic age, this analysis provided the promise of new strength and new popular support – only Labour ended the betrayals and marched back to principle.

The new left went straight for the jugular. Power was to be transformed by transferring it down to the activists. Policy would be formulated through the wishes of the activists coming up in resolutions passed by conference, then welded into a manifesto, not by the parliamentary party which had abused its independence, but by a National Executive dependent on the party activists. That manifesto would then become a binding mandate as the party was carried to power on it. It would be forced through by the votes of MPs, disciplined by reselection making them dependent on the constituency activitsts rather than on the patronage of leaders.

* *Manifesto*, 1981, pp. 105–6.

With such a discipline there would be no more betrayals, no more cuts, no more refusal to implement a manifesto which the mythology of the left told them was treated like a railway platform, useful for getting on the train but not to be taken on the voyage. To stop the rarefied atmosphere at the top of the tree fostering a Ramsay Macdonald syndrome assumed to be latent in all leaders, needing only watering by money and power to become incurable, the leader was to be elected not by the parliamentary party, which had always chosen him in the past, but by the outside party. Initially the left were vague about how this was to be done – conference was the preferred instrument but that meant domination by a block vote they detested and the real object was to pass more power to the activists. Yet as always method was treated as a subsidiary question. The principle was the important thing. The left preferred acceptance of popular principles to preoccupation with messy details.

Each of these changes could be readily justified in its own right particularly by reference to the new orthodoxy, 'democracy'. Each proposal had parallels overseas. Reselection was defended as obviating a conflict between member and local party which, in the Prentice affair in Newham, had become a species of trench warfare rather than a useful exercise in influence. It could be explained as ending neglect of constituencies of which there were several notorious examples among MPs too old, too indolent or too well cushioned by a huge majority to give their constituencies and their party the kind of attention more and more were coming to expect. Parties were no longer content to be a support system for an absentee MP. They wanted part of the action. Overseas members of representative assemblies and most Social Democratic MPs had to justify their tenure to their parties, usually through central control over the list. Similarly wider election of the leader was already practised by the Liberals, as it was by most continental socialist parties, few of whom elect the leader solely through members of parliament. Wider control of the programme was also common, though once again with a proviso that usually party membership was bigger and more active and hence had a greater claim to involvement and influence over MPs, party leader and party policy.

The problem was neither the antecedents nor the principle. It was the package. Eileen Short, delegate for Bethnal Green and Bow, summed it up at the 1981 Wembley conference:

> Comrades, we have already agreed on the method by which we will extend democratic control over the Labour Party by the rank and file membership and by the trade union movement. That control cannot be divorced from the conference decisions of the Labour Party. The experience of the last ten years, in particular the experience of the last Labour government – brought to grief on the rocks of the economic recession and the economic crisis that was rocking capitalism in Britain and throughout the world – and the experience of what happened to conference policies on which that government was elected, has meant that the Labour Party as a whole has determined that we need a change of policy, we need a change of programme and, if and when necessary, we need changes in our representatives and in our leaders. That is why we are debating these changes today.
>
> The party in parliament is there to represent the two arms of our movement, to give it a cutting edge in implementing the socialist demands of the resolutions and decisions taken by conference.*

The three items were inseparable, forming a new approach to party politics. They threatened an end to the independence of the Parliamentary Labour Party and the transformation of a party focussed on leadership which often seemed like a rusty bicycle likely to disintegrate unless it was ridden forward. It would become a more tightly disciplined vanguard party with MPs unable to preserve parliamentary independence by playing off party members against electorate and vice versa. The lines of authority were clear. And absolute.

* Wembley Conference, p. 145.

The campaign for the New Model began before the Callaghan government was beaten. At the 1977 Brighton conference a motion for re-selection was remitted to the NEC. When it reported back in favour of a 'Mikardo' compromise to provide for re-selection, not on a mandatory basis, but only when the constituency party wanted it, the proposal was carried by the conference but compulsory re-selection was rejected by 3,066,000 votes to 2,672,000 only because Hugh Scanlon 'forgot' to cast an AUEW vote mandated for compulsory re-selection. This near miss demonstrated how strong the pressure already was. So did the punishment of Ian Mikardo, thrown off the NEC in part for his compromise proposal. Strength was boosted by other factors. The 'betrayal' view was heightened by the manner in which the Callaghan government fell. As the Party General Secretary Ron Hayward put it in a bitter speech, as usual telling conference what it wanted to hear, 'Why was there a winter of discontent? The reason was that, for good or ill, the cabinet supported by the MPs ignored Congress and conference decisions. It was as simple as that, the Tories do it much better than we do. I wish our ministers or our prime minister would sometimes act in our interests like a Tory prime minister acts in their interests.'*

Apparently all would have been easy had inflation been allowed to let rip, though that would have meant ignoring other conference resolutions about the priority to be given to the battle on inflation.

The National Executive, long in opposition to the incumbent government, was freed by the fall of that government from any remaining restraints and decencies. In July 1979 it took a series of decisions allowing conference again to debate the principle of compulsory reselection despite a three-year rule designed to stop a continuous discussion of constitutional issues which could become all-absorbing. The party was not only to be encouraged to contemplate its constitutional navel, it was to be allowed to attack it with a screwdriver. The NEC also revived discussion of the new pattern for leadership elections and supported the principle of NEC

* Brighton Conference Report, 1979.

control of the election manifesto. The programme had been approved at the highest level, the defences against it were crumbling. The retirement of Hugh Scanlon meant an interregnum before the authority of the right was restored in the Engineers Union. The Transport and General was unmanageable, dominated by its left-wing executive ever since Jack Jones' democratic reforms. Others, such as NUPE, were noisily left, while still more were either inattentive to what was going on and particularly to its repercussions, or diffident about using their power. The left campaign was unstoppable.

The 1979 conference showed that only Labour Party inertia and the cock-up system of management could check the leftward tide. That conference, the tone, the bitterness and the hatred of MPs came as a shock to most, helped frighten and cow them. It created an atmosphere in which, thanks to the reluctance of the NEC to observe constitutional proprieties when they went against the interests of the left, all three elements of the programme were on the 1979 conference agenda and two were carried.

NEC Manifesto control	Carried 3,936,000 to 3,008,000
Compulsory reselection	Carried 4,008,000 to 3,039,000
Election of Party leader	BEATEN 4,010,000 to 3,039,000

Immediate victory was stalled only by reference of all constitutional issues to a 'Commission of Enquiry' initially proposed by the trade unions anxious to see they got value for their money but eventually accepted by the NEC on the proviso of a left majority. Potentially useful to delay or fob off, the 'Commission' did not in fact take minutes and waste years. It strengthened the clamour. Jim Callaghan and Michael Foot went to the crucial session at Bishops Stortford mandated by the Parliamentary Labour Party to oppose compulsory re-selection and resist a change in the leadership election. They were defeated on the first and bamboozled on the second; Moss Evans put forward the idea of an electoral college. Attractively weighted by giving the Parliamentary Party 50 per cent of the vote, it was sweetened by a proposal to use it to take the steam out of the campaign for changing the manifesto by making the college the final court of appeal on the manifesto. In practice this ill-considered idea would have involved the PLP in a greater mess than it ever had been in before, at the cost of creating a body so cumbersome it could not decide its own tea breaks, let alone deal with the complexities and compromises of a manifesto. Because they saw it as PLP-dominated, the left immediately opposed the college, which may be one reason why Callaghan accepted it. Yet on his return the PLP rejected it and those commissioned to draft the scheme failed to agree. Thus the Commission's idea turned damp squib. Yet the college was now launched, the unthinkable was being thought, particularly by the left who began to reconsider their first cool reaction. The college provided the means by which the battle for the leadership was won by the left. At the 1980 conference, variously described as 'absolute total bloody chaos' by Peter Shore and a 'slugfeast' by *Newsweek*, the new pattern of voting was:

Mandatory reselection	Carried 3,798,000 to 3,341,000
Election of Leader by College	Carried in principle 3,609,000 to 3,511,000
NEC Control of Manifesto	Beaten 3,625,000 to 3,508,000

The right was better organised, the results close. They were also largely accidental. The narrow majority on re-selection was due to the departure of the two leaders of the Boilermakers delegation to deal with a dispute (which they failed to solve) and the desertion by the delegation of the views of their executive. The narrow majority on the election of the leader was only won because the NEC opted for a decision in principle before the means were defined, an irresponsible device which worked, though conference then went on to reject the schemes of college composition put before it, largely because Terry Duffy insisted on casting his delegation's vote against them, to the anger of that delegation. Eventually it agreed to leave the decision to be agreed at a special conference once the NEC had come up with more acceptable proposals. The damage was done. The college was inevitable, won in the most discrediting way. The lid of the constitutional Pandora's box was, however, closed at last. Conference re-imposed the three-year constitutional reform. To do it now made reversal impossible.

Leaving bad situations to deteriorate makes them worse. Worse was the Wembley Conference of 24 January 1981. The right was confident it could win the least dangerous form of college: 50 per cent for the PLP, 25 per cent unions, 25 per cent constituencies. It was out-manoeuvred. Conference was tricked, in the way only shambling prehistoric beasts can be. It carried a formula no one had wanted in the first place and threw out the one most preferred.

The despairing right was committed to the simple solution of one man one vote. Since this could only apply to the constituency parties, and therefore took power away from the trade unions, it was not acceptable to a trade-union-dominated conference and was rejected with only 431,000 votes, Labour's equivalent of ignominy. The Parliamentary Party, the leader Michael Foot and moderate trade unions, such as the General and Municipal, were committed to 50 per cent, 25 per cent, 25 per cent. The National Executive had opted for one third/one third/one third. In a straight run-off between these two schemes the majority of votes would have favoured the first, leaving Labour a tenable, even workable, college and the PLP with the major influence and no possibility of a leader imposed from outside.

This common-sense solution was rejected. As the likelihood of their own scheme of one third each being rejected became clearer the left moved quickly. They began assiduously lobbying for an USDAW resolution to which the union had, more or less accidentally, got itself committed; a college divided 40 per cent for the unions and 30 per cent for the PLP and the constituencies. USDAW intended, once this was defeated, to support the PLP backed scheme. It thus became vital to stop withdrawal, which Clive Jenkins did by backing 40–30–30, then to rally behind it. Victory was assured when the AEUW delegation tied itself into a constitutional knot: having been mandated by a national committee determined that the delegation should not get out of control to vote only for schemes which gave more than half the votes to MPs, the AUEW delegation dropped out of the voting once their own proposal was beaten. The choice facing the left was summed up by the Blackburn delegate:

> Our votes will be cast for the USDAW proposal – 30, 30, 40. I am making no bones about this. There are three possibilities before you: the NEC's, the USDAW's, or the 50 per cent. The NEC's will not go through. Therefore really there is a choice of two. I will not mince words about what the choice is about. It is about power. It is about how much less power the PLP should have. Those who argue in favour of 50 per cent are asking us to trust our MPs in the way they vote. Shortly before Reg Prentice left to join the Tory Party these MPs voted Reg Prentice top of the poll for the shadow cabinet. (Applause.) In the elections last time they showed their contempt for most of the people in the CLPs by not even voting Tony Benn into a seat on the shadow cabinet. That is the attitude of the present PLP towards you. For those reasons I ask you not to vote for 50 per cent for the PLP.
>
> I come to a second point that has been touched upon, that is, that we should all unite. Unite behind what? I am prepared to see people like Owen and Williams and Rodgers leave the party. It is no use going into an election and winning by default against the Tories without a policy on which to operate, and the views of these people who are talking of leaving are so far removed from those of the rest of the party that they can play no part in our programme. I look forward to the time when Conference – next year hopefully – votes a binding manifesto upon the people who are going to draw it up, from the Conference or from the NEC.*

The NEC plan of a third/a third/a third was eliminated. The USDAW resolution was carried by 3,375,000 against 2,865,000 for 50–25–25. Michael Foot, who had courageously faced the first test of his leadership by giving no lead at all, now spoke up:

* Wembley Conference, p. 146.

I cannot pretend to you that absolutely all the results this afternoon were the ones I wanted . . . I agreed with the case put by David Basnett. I do not disguise from you, and I have not disguised from anybody, that I wish Conference had reached that conclusion . . . However, the Conference has made its decision and according to our constitution that is now part of our constitution. In accordance with those who become members of the Labour Party we accept the constitution. Therefore I certainly accept that vote, and I hope that the whole Party, without regard to Left, Right or Centre, will accept that vote as well. (Applause.) I say that in the interests of the Party as a whole, I believe that is the only way that we can properly and democratically conduct our affairs.*

The road to 1983 was open and clear ahead. It was a triumph of organisation, simple priorities and clear-headed determination over muddled thinking, diffident defence and an establishment which never really understood what it was defending or how to do it. It was also a public relations disaster. 'Has the change in the leadership system made you less inclined to vote Labour?' asked MORI. Less, said 30 per cent; more, said 5 per cent; 24 per cent thought the new election system better; 62 per cent thought it worse. 'Should the Social Democrats go or stay?' 'Go,' said 53 per cent, 'stay' 36 per cent. The parliamentary party had been divided and has never clearly formulated its views or made the consequences of change clear. The leadership had tried to fudge and fix and had seen every deal come apart only to make the situation worse. Luck had been with the reformers. In a long chapter of accidents with measures passed and then defeated, union delegations breaking ranks, misusing votes or tying their hands so tightly they could not move their brains, the story had all the elements of 'for the want of a nail'. Or a mind.

One final change remained: NEC control of the manifesto. This was carried at the 1981 conference by 3,609,000 to 3,400,000, after Michael Foot had warned the conference

* Wembley Conference.

that it would injure the relationship between PLP and party. The party then voted on the necessary constitutional provision and rejected it 3,254,000 to 3,791,000 since USDAW, mandated to vote for the principle but free to decide when it came into effect, had changed its mind.

The constitution of the party had been fundamentally changed. This had not been done by the two thirds majority sensible organisations would have required for major constitutional changes. That would have been beyond the capacity of the left. It was done by a series of constitutional fiddles, hairs-breadth majorities and cock-ups, all of which were made possible because the guardian of the constitution, the NEC, had not merely connived but rushed to facilitate the changes while the superintending angel, the unions, had had no idea of what was happening but were not averse as bargainers to getting a bit on the side for themselves.

The major change was in the position of the Parliamentary Labour Party. An independence vital if it was to do its job properly was now undermined. Parliamentary independence had certainly been abused in the past; abuse is implicit in privilege. MPs had used it as a cover for laziness, lack of attention to their constituencies, defiance of their constituency parties. It had led to insulation in the parliamentary club, an obsession with problems of government and parliament driving out wider concerns, a willingness to compromise things others regarded as vital, a propensity to give the old and tired freehold tenure in a comfortable cocoon. Whether these abuses were such as to discredit the greater good was a question never asked. The parliamentary party had to be able to lead and could not follow. It had to be able to compromise, diluting the fanatics' truth and adding flavouring and colouring matter to make it acceptable to the public. They were the sales force. They also had to govern, an art which requires choice. A team of denim-clad puppets could do the job the New Modellers wanted. Unfortunately it could neither win a majority nor carry on a governmental outward bound course like 1974–79. All this was never evaluated. The aim was to seize power, not run a political theory seminar.

This was the end of the maelstrom of change. Power could not be pursued any further. The effort had exhausted the party, but not the left. The inevitable divisive processes began. The right had organised in Solidarity another top-down group but more effective than CLV. The left's control of the NEC was slipping, and in 1981 five of its adherents, including Norman Atkinson and Margaret Beckett, changed from soft left to hard, and Bernard Dix (who joined Plaid Cymru in 1983) were replaced by right-wingers on the executive. Together with the break between Foot and Benn, which made Foot's supporters a balancing force, and the further shift in 1982 when Sid Weighell laid down his job to move the executive further right, this ushered in a new period of right dominance. Yet if the left could advance no further they could not be pushed back. The major damage was done.

Re-selection, the first change to be carried, was the most severe in its impact. Introduced as just one change rather than as what appeared to be a wider programme, operated in better times and with greater goodwill between a more successful parliamentary party and a more accommodating membership, it could have been manageable, even desirable. Such was not the climate. MPs were without honour in their own party, their efforts in keeping a government going with no majority regarded as a treason to socialism. They were corralled in MPs' seats at conference which at times looked like the accused dock at Nuremburg. The change satisfied ideology, possibly even democracy. Only human nature and practical politics were forgotten. MPs have to believe that their contribution to a job no one in their right minds would want to do has some value. They develop a certain self-importance necessary to keep going. Told that the party no longer wants him, it is a rare breed who will not find some excuse to see himself as right and those who turn him out as wrong. Wise parties allow personal ambition and party loyalty to point in the same direction and serve the same purposes. Labour had put them in opposition to each other. The result was predictable.

Forecasts were dire. 'Prentice sagas right through the country right up to the next election,' warned Joe Ashton, a situation which gave hope to those who wanted such a shake up to get into Parliament. Russell Proffit (who did not eventually make it) indicated clearly what was intended: 'The only way we are going to get alternative talent heard is to give them the opportunity at re-selections across the country and that is what we want. There are many people across the Labour Party who would like to be given the opportunity to represent it and all I am saying here today is, conference, you have the chance now to give them that chance.'*

In fact, only eight MPs fell victims to re-selection. John Sever, Eric Ogden, Ben Ford, Fred Mulley, Frank Hooley, Stan Cohen, Ray Fletcher and Arthur Lewis – none of them particularly impressive – while Reg Freeson managed to draw out the proceedings (aided by the incompetence of his local party) to escape his fate. Arthur Lewis stood against his replacement but most of the those deselected laid down and died for the party. Only Ben Ford, splitting the vote in Bradford North, lost Labour a seat. Yet many of the twenty six Labour MPs who defected to the Social Democrats, particularly in the later stages, must be added to the rejects. John Grant and Michael O'Halloran faced bitter battles in Islington; George Cunningham had won his but not by a majority he considered appropriate; David Ginsberg, Tom McNally, Jim Dunn and Dick Crawshaw would probably not have been re-selected and Neville Sandelson's difficulties with his local party were proverbial. Re-selection thus became a recruiting sergeant for the SDP and the SDP split subsequently lost fourteen more seats to the Tories. So a party which was already facing an uphill struggle and the loss of twenty seats in redistribution now took on the risk of split votes and an eventual loss of a dozen seats with a cheerful insouciance amounting to folly.

This was only incidental. The real consequence of re-selection was the blow to the self-confidence and efficiency of the parliamentary party. Labour MPs had to be given time off to fight their own battles in their own constituencies, then more time to fight them all over again and each other on redistribution. The sanction of re-selection with the party in its new mood hung over heads and made people more cautious about their votes on party matters. It created fear. MPs were already aware of the change in the mood of the party, even

* Conference Report, 1981.

their own constituency party. Yet, under the old procedure it was difficult for a constituency to get rid of its member. Some had tried, but with determined resistance battles were long: Reg Prentice had stayed until he had gone over to the Tories. Sir Arthur Irvine had shuffled on forever while his Liverpool Edgehill constituency fumed and fussed. Maureen Colquhoun had fought Northampton North over the objections of her party. An onus on the constituency party to incur the odium of acting against a member and pushing on through all the checks and barriers loaded the odds in his favour. Public sympathy was easily whipped up by an MP who could pose as bullied or badly treated. S.O. Davies in Merthyr Tydfil, Dick Taverne in Lincoln and Eddie Milne in Blyth had all successfully resisted such treatment winning their seats against their parties, though usually losing them later, while Eddie Griffiths in Brightside, perhaps the least worthy of all, won 10,000 votes in his attempt to stay on. Now all was changed. Re-selection was automatic. The onus was on the MP to organise to stay on. He had to become a faction leader in his own constituency. The debris of a bigger purge was less certain to be able to fight back and win sympathy. The whole balance of power had shifted.

Fear among the PLP led with the inevitability of a Greek tragedy to the next stage. Jim Callaghan's reaction to the Conference vote for a wider franchise for the leadership was to resign. Those on the left who had made his job so difficult promptly switched to persuading him to stay, but as usual he kept his own counsel and initiated an election before the new machinery could be trundled into place. Denis Healey was his obvious successor, a leader of standing, intellect and, as he modestly kept telling people, world reputation. The most popular Labour politician in the country, Healey had the common touch and the mind to belie it. He was also the most effective electioneer, master of the arts of television and people-pleasing. Within the party adulation was more muted. Combativeness had made enemies; he didn't suffer fools or ideological rubbish gladly. As former defence secretary and chancellor, he was identified with bombs, cuts, incomes policy and the final ignominy of the 5 per cent pay policy. All were crimes against humanity in the eyes of the left.

His opponents were Peter Shore, led to stand on the assurance from Michael Foot that he would not, John Silkin then, belatedly, Michael Foot himself, persuaded by pleas from party, unions and wife. Votes on the first ballot bore little relationship to their standing in the eyes of the public, which the Tory press kindly took the trouble to point out in advance.*

| | Party and Public Preferences | | | |
	Party		Lab voters	All electors
Healey	112	42%	68%	71%
Foot	83	31%	25%	16%
Silkin	38	15%	6%	9%
Shore	32	12%	1%	4%

The public preferred Healey. The party chose Foot. Few outside wanted him, many had a considerable antipathy: 30 per cent told Gallup he would be a good leader, 55 per cent that he would not, comparable figures for Healey being 64 per cent and 21 per cent. A third of the public told Gallup they would not like to see Foot leading the Labour Party, an odium exceeded only by Tony Benn, opposed by half the public. Among supporters of the party 40 per cent said that they would not like to see Tony Benn, 28 per cent Michael Foot, and only 15 per cent did not want Denis Healey, the man supposed to be both hated and divisive. Labour was so determined not to allow its choices to be dictated to by the polls that it perversely went directly against them.

The Conservative Party had behaved similarly in 1975. Then 29 per cent of the public and 36 per cent of party sup-

* *The Sun*, 3 November 1980. The Marplan poll, unfortunately a telephone survey, is the only one taken in the campaign. An NOP poll in the *Observer* (19 October 1980) showed 75 per cent for Healey, 19 per cent for Foot in a straight choice but that was before Foot's decision to stand. Another Marplan (7 November 1980) compared Foot and Healey with Margaret Thatcher in ability to deal with seven issues. Foot was ahead only on unemployment, Healey behind only on defence and world standing.

porters had preferred Willie Whitelaw as leader, with 13 per cent preferring Sir Keith Joseph and only 9 per cent (10 per cent of supporters) preferring Mrs Thatcher. Yet then 51 per cent of the public thought Edward Heath should go. In 1980 58 per cent wanted Mr Callaghan to carry on. Mrs Thatcher was regarded as an 'asset to the party'. Few objected to her in the way they did to Michael Foot for she had only a bout of milk-snatching to live down, Foot a long radical past as the man the press love to hate. Like the drip treatment in torture, such a process cannot go on for long without producing some results.

Labour ignored these facts. With Peter Shore and John Silkin both advising their supporters to vote for Foot, a decision at least one of them came to regret bitterly, the election was decided. Michael Foot was elected leader by 139 votes to 129. It was partly a stop-Healey vote from a party which had never felt a great affection for its loner non-leader. MPs were afraid to defy the growing chorus of the activists by electing him to take them on. Foot was installed as Labour's inglorious twelfth leader. His career was to be worthy of the thirteenth. One member of the shadow cabinet observed on leaving the meeting that Labour had decided to lose the next election.

It was an ostrich vote, the election of a talisman to protect from forces of evil raging through the land. Foot was seen by people such as the chief whip, Michael Cocks, as a man who could hold the party together, if only because of his ability to obscure the issues. A few like Neville Sandelson even voted for him as the surest way of weakening a party they now wanted to wreck. Yet in a party of Buggin's turn he was now Buggins and there was hope that the good old days would return by electing the good old leader. Indeed he had promised as much in a great Commons speech on 29 October:

> We shall organise the biggest protest campaign that this country has seen since the 1930s. We shall have a campaign from one end of the country to the other. We shall fight the government here in the house and outside. Shall we call it a Midlothian Campaign? It will be against the atrocities of unemployment this time instead

> of the other atrocities against which Mr Gladstone cam-
> paigned . . . We give due notice to the Conservative
> Party that we intend from this moment on to rouse the
> country from one end to the other to ensure that as soon
> as the opportunity comes we get not merely what we
> had for five years – a tender difficult situation with a
> majority one day and no majority the next – but the full
> majority to carry through the democratic socialist
> reforms that this country requires.*

The promise was to be partly fulfilled in demonstrations
which thrilled those taking part and alienated others, allowing Michael to orate, Denis Healey to be shouted down by
spitting images of Jon Lansman. Yet bringing heart to a
movement is different from winning hearts and minds. The
campaign petered out.

Michael Foot was elected as a sentimental gesture to him
and the party. He was trusted. He was still affectionately, if
not warmly, received at *Tribune* rallies. He had been the
rock on which the last government rested. He had radical
credentials albeit faded. Yet in looking for a lucky Foot the
party abdicated its duty to win. At 67 he was lame of gait,
weak of eyesight, curiously inflexible. He epitomised and
compounded all the problems of a party coming to be
regarded as old, out of touch and irrelevant. A television star
in the 1950s, he was hopeless in the personal interview situation of the 1980s, peering shortsightedly around, with a tendency to interrupt which alienated viewers, coupled with a
willingness to follow lines set by the interviewer instead of
seizing the initiative, obscuring issues instead of speaking
simply. Every attempt to tutor floundered in indifference. A
small group was set up to arrange television tutoring. It never
got beyond one question-and-answer session. Another group
was set up to popularise a diary filled with irrelevancies by
including factories, hospitals, schools. Nothing happened.
Michael liked meeting the party and reading books. Another
group was to act as brains trust for question time. It petered
out. Representations through Mrs Foot improved his appear-

* Hansard, 27 October 1980, pp. 608–9.

ance by a new haircut and suit. The week after both I sat next to him on the front bench and looked down to see odd socks. Margaret Thatcher as newly elected leader had set out to change her hair style and intonation, educate herself, travel the world, learn the techniques of the media and meet the people. Michael Foot had his hair cut; an endearing amateur in a job which demanded more and more professionalism.

None of this mattered too much except to affirm an image of irrelevance. What mattered was the style of leadership. Michael was never a natural leader. The wit and sparkle, the spontaneity of his oratory vanished under the weight of responsibility. In the gladiatorial contest of question time he was matched against one of the sharpest operators of recent decades with a fine line in moral indignation usually uttered while delivering a sharp knee to the groin. He fined down his questions from the hydra-headed approach to more simple points. He devoted more time to economics and got a tutor in it, Henry Neuberger from the Treasury, yet was still uneasy. He fought back but never mastered occasion or enemy. His oratory became long-winded phrasings and dated mannerisms. The inevitable position of a Labour Leader is respectability, leading the party to power and responsibility. Michael Foot half realised this but was still pulled to the left, still looked to old associates and old attitudes in an uncertain world though as out of depth with the new left as the old right. Every deputation which went to see him to urge that 'something be done' was greeted with a knee-slapping 'We must think about these things.' Then nothing happened. A lost leader, aware of the weight of his responsibility but unable to carry it, looking more and more inwards, to *Tribune*'s past and his own. He spoke to a young generation of Bevan, the health service, Neville Chamberlain, the great causes of yesterFoot.

To choose Michael Foot was to defy a reality which was getting harder. His poll rating began bad and got worse, lower than any leader since polling began, lower always than any of the depths Margaret Thatcher or any of her predecessors plunged in their worst moments. Some took refuge in defying reality with the kind of irrational arguments which were becoming strong in the party: previous leaders had

always been popular and Labour had still lost. Yet it does
not, therefore, follow that a leader who has to be dragged
along behind a party which is itself unpopular is a formula for
success. A Labour leader needs to run ahead of his party to
mediate between it and the public. As a party of change, of
the working class and the unions, Labour will always be
regarded with suspicion in a contented middle-class community, so the leader must offset this. Leadership popularity
does not bring victory. It helps a party which needs all the
help it can get.

None of these things were Michael Foot's fault. But they
were the faults of the leader the Labour Party had elected,
the man who was kept in power because each side needed
him against the other. To criticise a person is hurtful, though
that doesn't stop the process in a political party when everyone has to have a frank appraisal of everyone else's faults
since all are interdependent. To criticise a leader is more
impersonal, a matter of public record, since in the end he has
to perform certain inevitable functions. Michael Foot did not
and never could. He had other characteristics which inspired
other reactions. They were those of the man, not the leader.
He handled the party with affection and friendship. Most felt
affection for him. Yet it was protection for he was vulnerable. Television interviewers reacted in the same way, willing
to wound but yet afraid to strike, for kicking someone who
acted like one of them, who was so clearly vulnerable, was no
way to win friends and influence viewers. It was easier to do
the nice thing and let him waffle on. The effect was even
more destructive. Previous leaders had been set apart, Gaitskell by charm and presence, Harold Wilson by withdrawn
calculation, Jim Callaghan by dignity and sense of duty.
Michael Foot was human and frail and, because of it, protected to the extent of being cossetted. He never trusted the
right and the increasing attempt on the left to argue that he
was their prisoner made him trust them less. He had to work
with them; in practice his view of party and parliament was
similar, for he was bitterly critical of the anti-parliamentaria-
nism of the new left. Yet he only trusted his old friends, making his leadership the *Tribune* group in power at last. Too
late the opposition had arrived. It didn't know what to do.

Below the superficialities and the rolling waffle there was a hard kernel of obstinate ideology. The world no longer fitted it, so he sought protection from it through old cronies, building a team which was protection – Richard Clements from *Tribune*, John Evans as PPS, Norman Buchan, his old friend (of an ilk so similar that when I took him to the fishworkers' canteen on Grimsby docks, fishporters asked, 'Is that Michael Foot?') and the shadow cabinet's working-class representatives, Stan Orme and Albert Booth. A leader needs a team to link him to the outside world, to make him face the truth, to argue and to expose him to different views. Foot's team comforted, protected and agreed.

Michael Foot was the last leader to be elected by the system designed to choose popular figures. Election by the PLP had been the norm from the start of the party. Its responsibility is to mediate between the enthusiasts and reality. In 1980 they sought protection from the first and hid from the second. Abandoning responsibility, they were not given a chance to resume it. The change was made at the Wembley conference. The PLP, never enthusiastic about it, was slower to accept. In March they asserted their right to have the biggest say in the choice of leader by 144–24 with Michael Foot giving the lead and urging that the Wembley vote would be reopened at the October conference because it 'could not be regarded as satisfactory for the future health of the party'. It was the first of many promises.

PLP standing orders were in process of revision. The new provisions were included in a draft on 9 October 1981, with only fifty-five members present. Alan Williams' amendment to accept the new system for one session was accepted but when John Morris attempted to get the discussion postponed for proper consideration, Eric Heffer demanded it be withdrawn. If the standing order were not passed 'the media would only report that the wrangle inside the party on election of a leader and deputy leader was still going on.' By 23 to 32 chairman Fred Willey's proposal that consideration of that particular standing order be deferred was lost. The standing orders were accepted 'with the proviso that there was to be further discussion at a later date'. It never took place. The PLP, was delivered over, bound and gagged.

Whoever elected the leader determined the priorities of the party. The PLP was the section of the party most in touch with the public, the one component forced to look outward except when fear made it introspective, as it had done in the election of Michael Foot. To add other sections heightened party considerations, forced contenders to appeal more to the unions, the activists all those things which cut Labour off from the wider electorate. Contenders could still point out the consequences and the need to appeal to the people. Yet lectures win no votes and few candidates are successful by appealing to other constituencies.

The argument for the new system of leadership election was that it would strengthen the party, binding its sections firmly together. Its first consequence was to weaken Labour and produce recrimination between the sections. The inevitable result was a contest not for the leadership – both sides needed Michael Foot as a talisman against the other – but for the deputy. Tony Benn had been carefully building himself up as the leader of the left. He had kept clear of the 'illegitimate' election by the PLP, partly because he knew he would get nowhere in a party which had failed to elect him even to the shadow cabinet. Now his ambition and his greater strength in the new system had to be put to the test. An election followed, as night follows day, with the new system. It was also a useful change of ground, distracting the right from their first objective, reversing the constitutional reforms, to the more exciting battle of fighting over a non-job with no functions. The relevant strength of the two armies was to be tested in a personal jousting match.

The contest rolled on through a summer and autumn of trade union conferences, party meetings, television interviews and press rows. It discredited all concerned as well as the procedures by which it was conducted. There was no uniform decision-making process for the constituencies. Nearly sixty consulted all members, ten through postal ballots with high polls and more pro-Healey results than usual while others set up polling booths or ballot boxes at meetings. The rest took the decisions in the general management committees, 80 per cent of whom plumped for Benn. The unions fared worse, taking the decision on the basis of what method suited which candidate, rather than on any democratic or consistent basis. After being greedy for power they showed themselves incapable of handling it. Some, such as NUPE or the POEU, consulted their members and followed their preferences even where they were against the instincts of the leadership. Others, such as ASTMS, consulted conferences; some, such as ACTT, kept their largely Tory membership right out of it. One, the Transport and General, began a branch consultation which plumped for Healey, countermanded it by an executive decision for Benn, then left it to a delegation decision for Silkin. After a hole-in-corner meeting, the delegation then cast its final vote for Benn, choosing the worst of all worlds. And candidates.

The majority of the unions favoured Healey. The majority of their membership favoured him overwhelmingly. The great majority of the constituency parties went for Benn. The PLP was split. Seeing a vote for Benn would deliver him the election, sixteen *Tribune* MPs including Neil Kinnock, voted Silkin on the first ballot and abstained on the second. Four Tribunites switched Silkin–Healey and one voted Healey both times, while the rest voted for Benn. A half dozen members on the right voted for Healey and promptly left the party, causing Benn to claim moral entitlement to the deputy leadership since Healey's margin was 3.5 MPs. The final result was a tumultous majority of 50.426 per cent for Healey, a pathetic 49.574 per cent for Benn. The MPs, splitting 137 for Healey, 71 for Benn, decided the issue. Benn had dug his own grave with the PLP by the very technique which had built up his support in the party.

The election discredited Labour. It was an explosion of the pent-up bitterness and hatreds of the last few years. John Silkin fought an effective but irrelevant campaign but the intensity of feeling and passion of the others revealed publicly what had long been clear privately. The two sides in the Labour Party not only did not trust but did not even like each other. Labour was not one congregation in the broad church but two sects wrestling for control of the building. Tony Benn forecast that the democracy in action would be healing. It tore Labour apart.

The public have confused ideas of what parties are about

but the image they have centres on managerial competence
and effectiveness. A party is an instrument. People want it to
be able to do a job. A party which had become a mobile battleground manifestly could not. It was judged accordingly.
The scars within the party healed. Slowly. The impact on the
public remained. So did the one crucial consequence.
Because the electoral college was so cumbersome and divisive, because it could only be invoked at conference, Labour
was locked into Michael Foot. Had the proverbial bus come
along taxidermy would have been easier than an electoral
system with all the characteristics of a doomsday machine.

The third prong of the new model attack was control of the
manifesto. It lost in conference but won in every other
respect. The area had long been a disputed one. In the mythology of the party, conference decides policy but the parliamentary party decides timing and implementation. The two
have to be brought together in a Clause V meeting, to agree
on a manifesto which is usually a compromise. New
modellers wanted it to be clear, pristine and decided by the
outside party. Yet practicalities require compromise. Party
members are enthusiasts. They are in the party to get
change, to further causes. Governments are cautious, facing
the practical problems, particularly those of an economy in
decline where the system just cannot deliver. Leaders are
sensitive, anxious to please, reluctant to take unpopular
decisions, make alarming commitments. The tug of war is
perennial. Bitterness is inevitable. Yet the betrayal theory of
Labour governments, and particularly the last, now turned
what should have been a process of compromise and discussion into a zero sum game.

As the attack on the manifesto as a constitutional issue was
beaten off, the new left and the old were piling up further
policy commitments, taking by stealth what they had lost in
the frontal charge. Over four years the policy position of a
Labour government which had kept nuclear weapons and
decided to update them, accepted American bases, worked
within the Common Market, turned down a wealth tax, cut
government spending, sold off BP shares and tried to per-
petuate an incomes policy which cut the living standards of
working people was totally undercut. It was ruled out first by

the 'Draft' Manifesto authorised by the NEC in July 1980, and promptly disowned by the leadership then and in more constitutionally proper form by the policy statement *Peace Jobs Freedom* (carried by 5.2 million to 6,000, prompting a critic to ask whether the minority were voting for war, unemployment and slavery), which was the NEC's way of slipping through policies it wanted for its own reasons. Old government policies were made impossible also by a carefully organised campaign of resolutions, one by one closing the loopholes for the right.

Policy	Conference	Majority
No Cruise	1981	Majority, not two thirds
	1982	Two thirds majority
No Trident	1981	Majority, not two thirds
		Two thirds majority
	1980	Majority, not two thirds
No Polaris	1981	Majority, not two thirds
Non-nuclear defence	1982	Two thirds majority
No American bases	1980	Majority, not two thirds
	1982	Two thirds majority
Leave EEC	1980	Two thirds majority
No incomes policy	1978	Two thirds majority

Labour's policy processes are so inadequate as to be totally useless for a major party. Policy formulation is a complex process needing thought, preparation, documentation and discussion. Labour concentrates on a harrassed and ill-focused discussion carried on in public and distorted by a crude voting system. People who have had their hands tied by decisions taken months and years before in the light of different arguments and circumstances decide on what they haven't heard. Policy preparation demands a thought to saleability, the reactions of ordinary people and the problems of implementation. Labour concentrates on acceptability to the party assessed by crude rallying cries to the prejudiced, by slogans, and declamation. Useful policy demands a sensitivity to deep differences, an ability to navigate between shoals. Labour's processes force issues, generate confrontation and harden and entrench positions. Effective policy dilutes and generalises, concentrating on broad problems and wide-ranging appeals. Labour's processes provided a happy hunting-ground for pressure groups and enthusiasts of all kinds, though primarily for those with a left enthusiasm, such as feminist groups, racial groups and, above all, the old cause, now respectable and certainly growing in numbers and apparent strength, the Nuclear Disarmers. CND came back from the dead and was increasingly influential in the Labour Party.

Socialism is the language of priorities. In the Labour Party no one speaks it. The processes accumulate a shopping list of demands, taking everything on board irrespective of cost, practicability or acceptability. The process of policy formulation brought out all these faults in liberal measure then put them on prime time television for the nation to watch. The revolutionary socialists knew from past experience that infant lambs can face a ritual slaughter from a cruel and callous party butchers. They had to be protected and allowed to grow. This was the role of the National Executive Home Policy Committee and its chairman, Tony Benn. He should have been removed from that position after the 1981 conference as the NEC shifted right. Michael Foot, always anxious to conciliate, intervened personally to keep him on. The extra year was enough to complete the building of the paper Jerusalem. Tony Benn threw himself into a frenzy of policy work which fortunately kept him out of high profile politics for a year as he concentrated on formulating and strengthening the policy to make it impervious to right-wing counter attack.

The policy sub committees and groups of the National Executive are a jungle of ad hoc groupings, fifty in all, in which the denizens are an odd mixture of enthusiasts and cranks who usually attend regularly, experts, specialists, MPs who drift in and out, trade union representatives usually disenchanted, and Bennite ideologues who provide the impetus. They had been working at a slow, leisurely, pace, ploughing through 1,500 research papers and lots more remits and resolutions. Now time was shorter, the pace became more frenetic and the Home Policy Committee demanded documents for a Party Programme in 1982. A Bennite caucus moved from committee to committee pushing through decisions, which often had to be reversed or modified later. Intellectual scruples, those vast reservations set aside for the tribe of quibblers, were suddenly abandoned as group after group went through the conference decisions amplifying and illustrating and turned its work in to the Headmaster.

The concordance was *Labour's Programme 1982*, a guide book to Bennite Britain, incapable of fulfilment, giving every hostage to fortune, setting alarm bells ringing everywhere and attempting to square every circle: devalue but stop the pound falling, liberate the shop floor but plan centrally etc, etc. The whole was not so much a labour of love as premature ejaculation. It was also unnecessary. The party 'programme' is 'proposals adapted by conference by a two thirds majority', a long list of good intentions which is relevant only if items are taken out of it and inserted in the manifesto as agreed by NEC and Cabinet or Shadow Cabinet. In 1972, the NEC, for the first time, had actually pushed this further by publishing on a green paper basis 'for discussion within the movement' a programme which became in 1973 a 'full policy statement' which had not, however, been put to conference. In 1976 it had repeated this with a document which it had argued disingenuously was 'far more ambitious' than a manifesto and 'the essential background or the implementation of the manifesto itself' – a clear attempt to smuggle policies in by the back door when the front was constitutionally closed. Pushing ever forward the NEC had then put the document to conference which obligingly carried it 5.88 million to 122,000. It could do little else. The conference floor is not the place for unscrambling eggs, even addled ones. Now on the basis of these precedents the NEC revived the techniques with its monstrous 284 page *Programme 1982* adding with the usual slyness that 'the manifesto – given its usual length and format – is usually unable to include proposals or even guidance to cover the whole scope and detail of day to day government'. This was true. Yet it was not true that a document which had not gone through the full clause V procedure and which was therefore inferior to a manifesto could fill in the gaps and bind government hands even more tightly. This document was to be the basis for yet another innovation, a campaign document setting out 'the priorities over a five year parliament'. Yet first it had to be consolidated by putting the whole mess back to conference. The aim was to anticipate the manifesto, to tie the hands of the party and underline the policies for the rank and file by hardening the party's association with them. This put the onus on the right and the parliamentary party to justify any departure. But recirculated sewage is still sewage and repassage with the usual enormous majority hardly confers a new status to something which cannot really be discussed or analysed in a conference incapable of any higher thought than knee-jerk reactions. Nevertheless it was now 'the policies', a collective entity which stood, or fell, together, a checklist against which betrayals could be double-crossed.

Only resolute action by the Parliamentary Labour Party could have stopped the takeover. It could have done this by doing what it had done in the past and developing policy through the subject groups of the PLP, urging it in the House in opposition to the measures of Tory government. The lack of confidence of the parliamentary party, the distraction of reselection, the general collapse of morale, the lack of drive from the top and increasing strength of the new orthodoxy of Conference rules OK, all combined to sabotage any counter-attack. The PLP was not an effective force. Its subject groups were badly attended, hardly tied into front-bench leadership, concentrating on discussions and presentations by outside bodies and speakers, and falling down on the increasingly difficult job of rallying speaking teams. Only in three fields was there any counteraction. Roy Hattersley's team on home affairs began to develop a policy on race relations and urban problems in the face of the 1981 riots. Neil Kinnock's team on education set out to put firmer flesh on the skeleton. Most important of all, Peter Shore's finance team began to develop its own economic strategy and formulate it in the shape of a plan for growth and opposition budgets in 1982 and 1983. Shore's team incorporated conference policy but the thrust of their strategy was different, using expansionary Keynesianism and the dynamics of the market through devaluation as a stimulus to growth where the Alternative Economic Strategy was *dirigiste*, centring on controls, managed trade and the use of the power of the state. The Shore policies were effective and would have worked. They also provided an answer to the central problem of how to get growth, for without it everything else the party wanted was impossible. Yet they too were inadequate. They did not make the unions an offer they could not refuse to get collective action to restrain the inflationary consequences of expansion. The TUC had spoken with a forked tongue on incomes policy, paying lip-service to the principle, rejecting the practice. The Labour Party conference had been more ideological so the trade unions would go no further than a national economic assessment which they tended to interpret as power without responsibility, now the prerogative of activists as well as harlots. The only thing which would have given Labour's entire strategy credibility, a simple declaration that the unions would use their power to stop inflation taking off as expansion resumed, was never forthcoming. It was never even asked for by a leadership which regarded trade unions as sacred and was not prepared to bargain with them. Ask not what the unions can do for you was the attitude.

When he lost the chairmanship of the Home Policy Committee after the 1982 conference, Tony Benn's work was unfinished. It was completed by his opponents. John Golding as new chairman faced a dilemma. *Programme '82* was in no form that could be presented to the electorate. It had to be boiled down, diluted and interpreted into sense. Yet the demand for 'conference policies' was dominant in the party. The work of the Trade Union Liaison Committee, busily developing policy, albeit on similar lines, had also to be taken into account. The Bennite progress chart envisaged an innovation in Labour Party policy processes, a campaign document. The new majority played safe and continued the work. The campaign document emerged in March 1983 with a preface from Michael Foot talking of 'providing the essential background' for the manifesto and 'creating both the context and meaning of the manifesto commitment', another way of obscuring the constitutional balance between parliamentary party and conference. The document was focused on pleasing the party, a different perspective from that necessary for pleasing the people. Formulating a programme which is saleable and can be carried out is a very different process from papering over policy splits and splitting over policy papers.

It was still a long shopping list, cut down somewhat, but it is difficult to make a lawn by hacking down a jungle. Its proposals were mainly those of conference though Fudge and Mudge had played some part. On the Common Market caution had prevailed in a misguided attempt to appease; withdrawal was replaced by a commitment to negotiate out over the life of a government, exactly the wrong subject to compromise on since it simply invited a massive flood of imports as EEC competitors sought to forestall the axe. The overall appearance was that of a rag bag, some good bits, some bad, but no digestion and no sense of priorities or of how far policies could be multiplied without frightening electors. Gerald Kaufman was reported to have described it as the longest suicide note ever written. The right preserved glacial smiles. The left enthused. Its authors insisted on a new line; the answers were there. Invited to discuss it on radio, I talked to John Golding, intending to attack it. His reaction was of shock: it is the basis for rebuilding the economy. The gamekeepers had turned poachers because Golding is also a trade union man. When the unions have decided discussion stops. Being trapped himself, he closed the door on a party in the Bennite trap.

Private reactions were more hostile. Shadow cabinet members criticised the document in their meetings and privately to Michael Foot. They were reassured. It would not automatically become the manifesto. There would be a chance to discuss and change it. The spirit of Clause V, providing for joint discussions between shadow cabinet and NEC on the manifesto, would be fulfilled. None of the promises were kept. When Margaret Thatcher called the election John Golding and the party leadership faced a simple dilemma. To have attempted to alter the document with an election four weeks away would have opened up a can of worms which they had only just put the lid on. They accepted the inevitable. Change would have been regarded as a betrayal. It would have precipitated a major row from those who for four years had been preaching the sanctity of 'the policies'. Far better to go along and put the blame for failure on those who had foisted them on the party. The implicit assumption was thus that defeat was inevitable. The major question was blame. Perhaps the assessment was realistic but to have accepted the campaign document as the manifesto helped to make it so.

The left campaign to have the outside party control the manifesto triumphed, at the hands of their opponents. The right had no alternative. Shadow Cabinet discussion before the Clause V meeting between NEC and Shadow Cabinet was brief. The Clause V discussion lasted fourteen minutes; only Peter Shore demurred and his was more of a protest against the inevitable than an attempt to stop it. At the PLP meeting afterwards criticism was muted. George Robertson attacked the document's position on defence as being not only contradictory but dangerous. He was roundly denounced for rocking the non-nuclear boat. Ann Taylor and Ken Woolmer criticised the document as too long and detailed but there was little anyone could do. 'New Hope' was overwhelmingly accepted. Labour was to enter the 1983 elections with the most radical set of policies of any European socialist party, a manifesto which contained 13,000 words in contrast to the Tory Party's 10,000 words. Our words were solid lists of demands. Theirs were explanations, conciliations and evasions, carefully construed formulae to obscure the reality to come. We thrust unpalatable truths at the people. It was the red meat of socialism, packed with enriching vitamins, and as such was totally unsaleable to a frightened electorate anxious about Britain's decline, puzzled about the reasons and worried about the alternative. It was certain to be exploited by a government that now had nothing to offer but fear and was certainly going to proffer that in full measure. So Labour provided the raw material for the process of fear creation which became a central part of the 1983 election. So much raw material in fact that the Conservatives and their propagandists only needed to take a few shots out of crammed lockers.

In four years the party had been new modelled. The structural changes imposed shackles on a party already arthritic. They reduced the party's effectiveness as a machine for winning elections without actually making it a more perfect democracy. Dave Nellist, Militant supporter, foretold that 'If I could go to a worker and his or her family in the streets of Coventry and say, "You join the party, you decide the policy in the democratic measure in the party and then you know it is going to be carried out by the party leadership because it is mandatory on them" I am sure we could go out and recruit thousands of workers to the party, thousands of families into the Labour movement' (1980 Conference Report). In fact membership fell; 348,156 in 1980, 276,692 in 1981, and up to 278,327 in 1982. The mass party was dying on fewer feet. It was more democratic only in the sense that another wing controlled it. It was also a less attractive party to be in, characterised by continuous argument, bullying, intimidation, and a general rejection of that old fuggy indifference once called comradeship. The party faced a more crucial election with a machine which was substantially weakened.

The reforms were a result of concentration on the party's own problems. Labour was preoccupied with itself, becoming more and more introspective, taking on more and more of the characteristics of a sect, less and less those of a great shambling, permeable, outward-looking party. Ideology typified the change. In the 1950s the party had been 'Labourist', dominated by the trade unions, their practical preoccupations as well as their sacred cows. By the 1980s, sound ideology was the fashion. The *New Statesman* had gone from good writing to sectarianism like *New Socialist* and its clientele: ideologues writing for each other about Marxist economics, Marxist sociology, feminism and race. About how to win the election it said nothing, though a few real Marxists – Stuart Hall, Eric Hobsbawm – were allowed in to warn that the sectarian rigidities of the left were the omen of decline. No one else had that much practical sense. Sectarianism is self-selecting, self-reinforcing, self-rigidifying.

It was also self-deluding. Tony Benn, leader of the new modellers, assured them that Labour was on its way to victory. The prime minister and her allies in business, the city and the press were beginning to panic.

> For they now realise that the Labour Party could win a landslide victory at the next election. The present campaign for democracy and socialism within the Labour movement has given hope to millions of people who have sunk into despair because of unemployment, the destruction of our wefare state and nuclear-war-mongering . . . the decay of capitalism is the real reason for the crisis which is now destroying our industry and welfare state, undermining our democratic institutions and endangering world peace . . . We are demanding a return to full employment and the expansion of essential public services. We are demanding equal rights for women and ethnic communities, full rights for trade unionism, a freedom of information act, an end to the House of Lords. We want a new structure for European cooperation that will bring Britain out of the Common Market. We want a non-nuclear defence strategy and the removal of all American nuclear bases from Britain. If the Labour Party in parliament, and throughout the country, unites around these policies they will win massive public support. That is why the Tory press is now attacking us so violently. They know that if Labour campaigns as a team for these policies, Mrs Thatcher will be swept from office . . . If we keep faith with those we represent, and if we keep our nerve, there is nothing that can stop us from restoring our society to a new and fairer basis . . . The greatest problem we face is not that our policies are unpopular. The problem is that many people don't believe what we say and don't know whether we would do it if we were elected.*

* *Guardian*, 5 September 1981.

4 · Men Overboard

Those whose suave slick manner now leads them through TV studios and drawing-rooms just as it once led them through local Labour Party selection conferences have destroyed the trust between the PLP and the party which has to be so painfully built up again.

ALEC KITSON

A political party in a two-party system responds to basic laws. It must drive to the amorphous centre, gathering votes alienated by the other party to build a broad majority. It must avoid splits in both its own vote and the vote against the other side, a trick learned early by the Labour Party which formed an electoral pact with the Liberals before the triumphant election of 1906. The desertion of 'National Labour' and its effects on the real version underlined that lesson in 1931. It was also written into the constitution. Candidates for nomination bind themselves to support the party's choice, a restraint on taking disagreements into a public contest certain to harm the party. Individuals advance their careers through the party or not at all, becoming so dependent on it that only a massive dose of hubris could make them kick over the traces.

Thus party management is a fine art of keeping groups working together in broad coalition. Yet that process becomes increasingly difficult as new problems and complex issues make parties more fissiparous and cut across basic loyalties. The Common Market cut across the left–right dimensions. So did incomes policy and even defence, particularly attitudes to nuclear weapons. The failure of governments to deliver on public expectations, the increasing recourse to high interest rates, cuts and defence of sterling,

all required a new calculus, particularly in the Labour Party.
Which was right: to defend the government for the greater
good or take a stand on the issues? Moral issues – hanging,
abortion, homosexuality, drugs – could not be managed on
party lines. Yet as society became more sophisticated they
assumed more importance. The old red mare she couldn't be
what she used to be.

A sensible response was to hold the reins more loosely, to
treat the party like its American counterpart as a looser
coalition, a holding company for the similarly minded; to
concentrate on broad lowest common denominators, not
specifics. The new left's priorities were different. They had a
different view of party and reality. They looked to a party
united on the issues, a tighter discipline and the MPs as
agents of the party line. This ran contrary to the self-importance and the self-image of MPs, to the trend of the times and
to the complexities of a more pluralistic society. It therefore
made Labour more brittle, generated resentments and
increased the likelihood of a split.

The outlines of that split were emerging. The fault lines
were there, though their pattern was initially confused. One
set led outwards from the Jenkins epicentre. His differences
with the party he loved less and less went back a decade to
the bitter arguments over Common Market entry which had
led to his own sulky resignation as deputy leader and to his
leadership of sixty nine Labour MPs into the lobby to vote for
membership, thus enabling the Heath government to carry its
measure. Over the years Jenkins had gathered a small but
devoted following of worshippers, former associates and
admirers which lavished enthusiastic support on him. They
were an exclusive coterie on the right of the party, so far to
the right, said Tony Crosland, that many had disappeared
over the horizon. Europe symbolised this. It was not only a
passionate commitment but an abdication. Crosland and
Jenkins both knew that the 1964–70 Labour government had
failed economically. Crosland turned, in *Socialism Now*, to
an attempt at explanation and regeneration in socialist terms,
just as Stuart Holland and the left were doing in terms of a
different socialism. Jenkins and his supporters turned to
the EEC. Access to a wider market and hitching Britain's

flagging economy to the faster moving growth engines would redress the failures of a nation state which they were giving up hope of ever jolting forward on its own. The implicit assumption was that Labour did not have the answers and Britain could not make them work. Salvation had to come from the outside. So Europe represented a substantial move to the right. Personal pique pressed in the same direction. Jenkins was aggrieved by the party's hostility to Europe, which led him in pique into giving up the deputy leadership, at the failure of the party to respond to his resignation and even more at his small vote in the 1976 leadership election. He pulled out of a Labour Party increasingly unworthy of him and departed to Europe unloved and unlamented. No sad song of 'will ye no come back again' rose to the prince across the water. So the gap became a gulf. David Marquand, his old disciple, first revealed how far it had widened in an article, 'Inquest on a Movement', after the 1979 defeat. The implicit assumption was that social democracy was dead, killed by a reaction against it from the working class it was meant to serve. They were repelled by the structures of control it had erected, alienated by the unions, hostile to the burden of taxation required by growing public spending. Yet rather than defer to its natural leaders, the 'radical intelligentsia', who had always played such an important part in the development of its ideas, the modern Labour Party spurned its natural think tank. It neither wanted, nor was it able, to revise its assumptions.

> Both these failures – of will and of capacity – had their origins in a strange inward-looking proletarianism which became increasingly prevalent in the parliamentary party and in the party headquarters in the late 1960s and 1970s and whose proponents imagined that the 'Movement' had no need of ideas or intellectuals and could rely exclusively on the strong arm of the working class. It was a mood, not an ideology, this proletarianism, a smell in the air, not a text in paper . . . At the first level it takes the form of what might be called the 'cult of the tea-room', a defiant assertion of a (frequently bogus) working-class identity: an equally

defiant rejection of what are seen as middle-class values and middle-class models of behaviour . . . At the same time the 1970 defeat suggested – or at any rate was thought to suggest – that the party needed the unions much more than it had imagined . . . the party had lost because 'our people' had deserted it: because traditional working-class voters, alienated by wage restraint and anti-union proposals, had stayed at home: in other words because the party leaders had had the temerity to differ with the trade union establishment which understood better than the party did what made working-class voters tick. This alternative explanation was made still more plausible by the victories of 1974 . . . The proletarianists, it seemed, had been proved right: and right electorally as well as emotionally. The clever people, the intellectuals, the claret-drinkers, the barristers, the academics, the frequenters of London clubs, the article-writers and television-appearers, with their glib phrases and their disloyal attitudes, their outside interests and their European friends, had been shown up. The party did not need them after all.*

This was something more than an ideological alienation, it was a social gulf, one in which the 'intellectuals' or at least the Jenkins variety, felt neglected and rejected. The warning was clear.

Political allegiance is a matter of emotional loyalty at least as much as of conviction and my emotional loyalties are to the Labour Party. I would find it horribly painful to have to accept the notion that it has now out-lived its usefulness: and although I can see that the facts point in that direction I still hope that by some miracle the party can return to its old vocation as the chief vehicle of radical reform in this country. But the chances do not seem to me good.†

* *Encounter*, July 1979.
† Ibid.

It was a one-sided statement, taking no account of the scramble of at least two of those intellectuals to Brussels, losing crucial seats in the process. Instead of fulfilling their responsibility as intellectuals, to analyse why growth failed, and to provide a social democratic alternative to the *dirigiste* 'Alternative Economic Strategy', as Crosland would surely have done, these intellectuals merely wrote growth off urging as an alternative a new libertarian, decentralist society which seemed more likely to benefit the middle classes than the workers Labour had traditionally looked to. The underlying assumption was one of distaste for an unmanageable, irrational working class and its clumsy, lumbering unions so selfishly determined to benefit themselves in a way 'radical intellectuals' never do. Britain was failing because its workers and its unions were.

Absence made the heart grow cooler. Roy Jenkins returned in November 1979 to give a Dimbleby lecture which became an extended party political for a party which did not yet exist. Where the acolyte had hinted, the master made it clear that his thinking was moving in the direction of a new centre party to occupy the centre ground and introduce stability into a system which two-party politics were destabilising. It would mobilise not other old rejects but people of 'talent and goodwill' who had been alienated by the follies of the existing parties and system. He followed this in June 1980 by a speech to the parliamentary press gallery, the media establishment once again concerting action against Labour, by comparing the centre party idea to a plane which might 'well end up a few fields from the end of the runway, but the reverse could occur and the experimental plane soar into the sky', a clear application for the pilot's licence. Labour's old bus was no longer comfortable or convenient.

In American mythology the middle of the road is characterised by a litter of dead skunks and a long yellow streak. A June 1980 MORI poll asked people if they would be likely to vote for a centre party if formed. 'Very' or 'fairly likely,' said 30 per cent. 'Unlikely,' said 57 per cent, youth being more attracted than age, Labour voters more than Tory. The position was not particularly comfortable for those already there. It had produced alternating hope and frustration for the Liberals, with the big breakthrough in either votes or seats constantly hoped for, constantly postponed. The 'Liberal vote', far from constant is built on shifting sands. David Steel felt this frustration more acutely than other Liberals. He alone was capable of playing in the big league, yet the company he kept relegated him to kindergarten politics. He was, therefore, anxious to break through to the left, to add new forces to a Liberal Party which appeared to have run out of steam. Jenkins seemed to offer than opportunity. More of a social democrat than the rest of his party, Steel was perfectly amenable. Discussions between the two began and continued intermittently, centring not so much on a new party as on recruiting Jenkins for the Liberals.

Other creatures were stirring in the forest. Shirley Williams, always one of Labour's most attractive features, and a strong public preference for leader in 1976, had unexpectedly lost her seat in 1979, a traumatic blow since it coincided with personal losses, divorce not the least of them , to unsettle and take her out of the mainstream. Roots in the parliamentary party which would have kept her more stable, more in touch with reality, were cut. Just how out of touch she had become was indicated by her own proposal that Labour should welcome Roy Jenkins back and offer him a senior position in the party when his period as president of the Commission ran out at the start of 1981.

Bill Rodgers, always on the right of the party, was like Marquand, increasingly disillusioned about the traditional staples of social democracy and worried about big government: not more spending but better spending was his aim, not more government but more efficient. As defence spokesman of a party which was now moving in a unilateralist direction he was increasingly exposed, finding the new membership in the constituencies more and more immune to his traditional skills of organising, fixing, building up opinion in the way he had in the similar crisis from 1961. This feeling of alienation was heightened when Michael Foot, after Rodgers had been re-elected to the shadow cabinet, instead of dividing the emerging defectors by buying one off, gave good jobs to his friends and offered Rodgers nothing.

Rodgers resigned. Less intellectually at odds but more impatient was David Owen, all bustle and shining ego, a young meteor currently stalled. He suffered from an Oswald Mosley syndrome. Like Mosley, his ambition and his ego were too big for a pedestrian party, the plodding ways of a Labour Party, which not only did not defer to excellence but actually frustrated it.

The preoccupations of this group were different. They still saw themselves as fighting a rearguard action to save the party Jenkins had given up on. Their instincts were still Labour, albeit right wing. He hovered above it. Yet there was a mutual admiration and intermittent contact, and all showed a common enthusiasm for the European Common Market as a matter of religious faith. The commitment to leave made at the 1981 conference was even more unacceptable to them than the change in the mood or the decision on reform and re-selection. Shirley Williams, who had pointed out in June 1980 that 'a centre party would have no roots, no principles, no philosophy and no values', was coming round to the point of view she expressed at conference in October: the possibility of leaving the party if it resolved to withdraw from the market.

Events were bringing the Labour dissidents together to do just that. They staked their claim on 1 August 1980. They warned that Labour was facing the gravest crisis in its history, set out where the party was going wrong in policy terms and concluded that, though they would not support a 'centre party', 'if the Labour Party abandons its democratic and internationalist principles, the argument must grow for a new democratic socialist party to establish itself as a party of conscience and reform committed to these principles' (*Guardian*, 1 August). The warning was clear. Twelve Manifesto Group MPs (seven of whom were later to desert) called in September for reform of the party and a loosening of the trade union domination, and warned that Labour might face competition 'from Social Democratic Alliance Candidates, from sitting MPs dislodged by the re-selection process and perhaps from a new centre party'.* The mountain now came

---

* *The Times*, 22 September 1980.

to the new Mohammets. Roy Jenkins was in close touch with his committed followers in the PLP, both Lords and Commons, and the Gang of Three. He and the gang met on 18 January to prepare for the Wembley conference and a split they were ready for. A third small group of the alienated was more disparate but included Neville Sandelson, back in the Commons over the opposition of his constituency party, whom he described as 'half-wits', and determined now to throw every possible spanner into the works, which got him called the 'kamikaze' MP. He openly supported the Social Democratic Alliance, led by Stephen Haseler and Douglas Eden, and had taken every opportunity to be traitorous to Labour, lambast the NEC and poke fun at Labour sacred cows, as in the reply to his constituency party secretary who invited him to attend the picket line at Grunwick: 'Dear Sir or Madam, I am sure the police can manage without my assistance.' Also disillusioned were Tom Ellis, MP for Wrexham, ready to leave alone or with others; John Horam, Rodgers' old ministerial associate (prompting the joke, 'Have transport, will travel'), a front-bench spokesman but increasingly alienated by Labour's drift away from the market socialism which was the basis of his philosophy; Robert MacLennon, cautious, canny and watching; and Tom Bradley, who never said much, or indeed anything, but who would go wherever Jenkins indicated. They and others had already met informally. Some had met David Steel, not to join the Liberals ('I wouldn't have dreamed of doing that,' said Sandelson) but to explore the possibility and prospects of a breakaway and Steel's reactions to it. They were favourable, but Steel doubted the status of those behind it. There was nevertheless a drift to acceptance that something was going to happen. Sandelson, who had written out his resignation in February 1980, was persuaded by Horam and Rodgers to wait for the Labour conference, which they all knew would be a watershed.

Outside parliament there was the Campaign for a Labour Victory, formed in 1977 but a pale and inadequate shadow of the Campaign for Democratic Socialism which Rodgers had organised in the early 1960s. This had the support of 100 MPs and several right-wing unions, including the GMWU and

AUEW, and included on its 3,000-strong mailing list, filed in
the EEPTU computer, the respectable right of the party in
both unions and constituencies. Yet it lacked effective organisation and cohesion, and had no backbone except the
newsletter. It was more an elite façade than an effective
organisation for fighting the tides of change within the party.
Indeed it was to become more effective as a campaign for
Labour defeat.

This organisation was now thrown into a rearguard action
to try to stop the inevitable electoral college by a call for a
party democracy of one man one vote. Too late. The proposal was an ill-prepared and belated response to the growing strength of the left. David Owen began to urge it
vigorously but it had no hope of success because it compounded defeat by taking on two unbeatable opponents, the
unions, who would be deprived of a role in a party-member
ballot, and the activists, by depriving them of their power in
the constituencies. Right in principle, 'one man one vote'
was put forward as a popular symbol, not a realistic possibility: a good issue to leave on. This was certainly David
Owen's approach. He had come to the conclusion that the
struggle within the Labour Party was hopeless, the ground
for a break had to be planned by a strategy which made
Labour look as bad as possible, the defectors as good.

Thus everything was prepared for a break. The media, or,
more accurately, those pundits originally sympathetic to
Labour, cossetted and encouraged it, continually urging its
justification, boosting the confidence of those venturing out
on to the sea of troubles. Media and middle men needed
each other. And deserved each other. The signals were set
for go, the plans prepared, the media briefed, the minds conditioned. When their proposals (inevitably) lost at the
Wembley conference a whole organisation was ready to be
trundled into action. The Limehouse meeting and the declaration – basic Butskellism better written by Roy Jenkins,
the personification of a better yesterday – followed, not as an
angry response, but as a carefully prepared next step, a piece
of brinkmanship which led inevitably to the cutting of the
umbilical.

Bets were hedged. The Council for Social Democracy

could have existed within the Labour Party, for it was a compromise between Roy Jenkins' original conception of a revived centre and the Gang of Three's new sanitised Labour Party, though now with a break clearly foreshadowed.

> The council will represent a coming together of several streams: politicians who recognise that the drift towards extremism in the Labour Party is not compatible with the democratic traditions of the party joined by those from outside politics who believe that the country cannot be saved without changing the sterile and rigid framework into which the British political system has increasingly fallen in the last two decades . . . We recognise that for those people who have given much of their lives to the Labour Party the choice that lies ahead will be deeply painful. But we believe that the need for a realignment of British politics must now be faced.*

The Council already had the adhesion of ten MPs, obvious dissenters, loyal Jenkinsites and those such as Robert Mac-Lennon, whose Highland cunning led him to play his cards so close to his chest that he continued to insist on fightback tactics at the Wembley conference only to emerge next day as a deserter. It had also prepared its way in the country by using the CLV contacts. On 5 February a list of a hundred supporters was published. Perhaps the most impressive were Clive Wilkinson, Labour leader in Birmingham, Frank Chapple of the EEPTU, both of whom later stayed with the Labour Party. This called for further recruits to send in names and donations – £80,000 came from 30,000 people. A party within the party was emerging, the embryo for a break which quickly became inevitable. They hadn't gone. Everyone knew they were going. In background briefings they had said as much but they still hoped to be pushed rather than facing the indignity of jumping. As Phillip Whitehead put it, it was 'marsupially ensconced in the Labour Party ready to pop out of the pouch once the local elections are past.'†

---

* Limehouse Declaration, *The Times*, 26 January 1981.
† *Listener*, 29 January 1981.

Right to the end, and after, Shirley Williams hovered and
hesitated, Bill Rodgers was doubtful, reluctant to break a
lifelong association but thinking it his duty. Yet David Owen
and Roy Jenkins were absolutely clear-minded for a break
which in their heads had already happened, though each
envisaged different consequences. David Steel was prodding,
pushing and levering from the outside. Michael Foot
appealed to them at the Wembley conference to stay and met
them to urge the same. Yet a leader who had already lost
could offer nothing but the endless labour of being beaten,
with abuse as a bonus. Thus the pressures for a break were
remorseless. Shirley Williams resigned from the NEC on 9
February. In March twelve Labour MPs resigned the party
whip.

The left were delighted, wanting the gang to go forth and
not multiply. On the right there was sadness. Shirley Williams, ever loath to face unpalatable reality, continued to
deny that she was going, even after she had gone, creating
feelings of betrayal by trying not to hurt. Her own mood was
one of 'when shall we three, or four or more, meet again?'
David Owen, after an unusually bitter last attendance at the
Manifesto Group, argued that they shouldn't fight – 'one day
we'll have to come together again.' 'I'll never stand against
you. It's something I've got to do but I'd never fight you.
We've got to stay friends,' said the Grimsby party secretary,
one of the original hundred signatories, to me as he prepared
to leave to join 'another socialist party'. 'You have one of the
best constituency MPs in the country. Take pleasure in his
achievements, comfort him in adversity,' he wrote to the
Grimsby GMC, emotions and promises repeated all over the
country. Both were transient. By 1983 the former Grimsby
Labour secretary was the Grimsby SDP candidate and writing in his leaflets, 'What has the last MP done for Grimsby?
Consider his record, not his promises.' The sadness was
mainly manufactured. The world which was falling apart had
never got on particularly well together. The break was not a
great party split like 1931 but a public relations event. Real
feelings were deader. The mood was one of inevitability, as
if a formal decision long taken was merely being ratified.
Public relations allowed for a show of sadness but their sheer

dominance drove out the substance. Auld acquaintance were not only soon forgot but bitterly hated.

Secession has a logical progression. Yet bitterness was slow to develop. Though Tony Benn demanded loyalty oaths to make everyone live up to his own loyalty standards, the right were not yet prepared to attack old colleagues, while the left were not displeased. The steady drip drip drip of other defections, bringing both the dribs and the drabs to a dingy procession as other MPs deserted for a whole series of less clear-cut and mostly less worthy motives, delayed hostilities. So did Labour's intense preoccupation with the deputy leader election. The party was too busy at war within itself to wave goodbye. Moreover it was not yet clear what was being hatched. The SDP was a strengthening of the radical centre for Roy Jenkins, a new and better Labour Party for David Owen and Shirley Williams, who described themselves as 'the inheritors of the old Labour Party', an organisational challenge for Bill Rodgers, a life raft from a sinking ship for some who had scrambled aboard to avoid re-selection, and a Catholic party like Australia's DLP for others. One thing they could not be was another Liberal Party or, as Tom Forrester, an SDP defector from Labour, put it, 'a rubbish transfer station for all other parties'. The Liberal job was hitting out impartially to left and then to right, anti-Tory when the Conservatives were in office, anti-Labour when Labour was in, but always marching a mass of idealism, and an even greater mass of protest votes, into that dead-end street into which a first-past-the-post electoral system condemns third parties. That was not how rather superior new people saw themselves. They might be wandering into Lilliput but they took Gulliver's frame of mind.

The Liberals were a body of individuals posing as a party. Each MP owed his election to his own efforts. In parliament it was convenient to trade under the same label but this did not make them a party with a clearly defined set of attitudes and responses because they had no social base. The Liberals were inexperienced in government, highly experienced politically. The SDP were ministers in search of a party. The Liberals were anti-big government, the hairy men, quirky in pursuing such fetishes as site value rating. The SDP were the smooth men, instinctively governmental in attitudes and in thinking. Liberals were pavement-pounders, the SDP big-thought thinkers and talkers. The Liberals were against the system. The SDP were part of it. Liberals saw themselves as the centre. The SDP, with the exception of Jenkins and his clan, saw themselves as on the left and even he claimed to be 'radical centre'. Their main antagonism was directed at the Labour Party. They had to justify their desertion by attacking it, portraying it as irredeemable. Indeed the more clear-eyed, such as David Owen, appreciated clearly that they had to destroy Labour. A third party could not break through to majority status unless it destroyed one of the major parties or one of them fell apart. Labour had broken through with the Liberal Party split. A similar breakthrough was the only avenue open to the SDP and the only candidate for destruction was Labour. So like most converts they concentrated the bulk of their fire upon their old church, and their attacks grew more bitter and frenzied in inverse ratio to the fading away of Labour's internal war.

It is the job of the alternative government in a two-party system to mobilise discontents against the government and use them as the drive for its own rise to power. A third party hampers this process by syphoning off discontent. It can best do this at by-elections when the issues are less important, reality less oppressive and escapism more attractive. Yet the Liberal by-election upsurge of 1972–73 had been followed by a general election slippage as the electorate faced the issue of government in crisis rather than being able to register a harmless negative protest. In the 1979 parliament the Liberal Party had remained in the doldrums, its support below 10 per cent, with no indication of any stirrings in by-elections. The same thing had happened initially under the Heath government, so there was still the possibility of a new revival from the end of 1981. Yet it was not inevitable. What had worked once might not work again. The electorate could become disillusioned with failed hopes as well as failed governments. Certainly the Scottish Nationalists, fuelled by the same discontents from 1970–74, were not only in the doldrums now but remained there. That fate could have been in store for the Liberals – as well as the same splits. Yet now the defectors gave them a new boost and a new credibility, enlarging the bucket into which protestors could spit. They made the third party look new and hence once again workable. They bought new and popular faces, and their bitterness inflicted incalculable harm on Labour. Many who still thought of Shirley Williams, Roy Jenkins and David Owen as 'something to do with the Labour Party' assumed the war between the SDP and Labour was simply a continuation of the bitter internal argument in the party. As indeed, in a way, it was. The image of Labour disunity was amplified and perpetuated.

The departure of Shirley Williams, David Owen and even Roy Jenkins made Labour less attractive and a different party. Support had come back to Labour after the 1979 defeat because the policies of its government looked more credible as Margaret Thatcher's promises were discredited, its people looked more solid and trustworthy by contrast with what followed. It was a feeling of 'Come back, Jim, all is forgiven'. The developing split and the change in Labour's tone and leadership prevented its capitalising on continuity and took away the Jim factor while leaving Jim, for the SDP claimed the Callaghan mantle, and Labour busily tried to make itself different. The less attractive figures, the Skinners, the Heffers, the Benns, now loomed larger in the depleted Labour ranks.

Everywhere people who identified with the politics and personalities of the deserters went too. So did people who had never liked the trade unions and never sat easily in a proletarian or increasingly polytechnic party. The Fabian Society, most vulnerable because most respectable, had over a hundred resignations, but Fabians are too genteel to make a great exhibition. The real fall was from 3,502 members in 1980–81 to 2,600 in 1982–83, not an outflow but a flood. In the media Labour supporters who used their positions to invent the new party – Peter Jenkins in the *Guardian*, Adam Raphael in the *Observer* – and lesser imitators started pronouncing the death of the Labour Party, building up a vested interest in proving their own hypotheses. As well as the political weeklies, the intellectual periodicals, *Encounter*, *London Review of Books*, the quality press all gave disproportionate coverage to the new party, presenting it in the most favourable limelight, elevating it from opportunism and accident to a genuine contribution to political theory and new politics. All over the media disillusioned Labour men boosted the SDP as a symptom of their own alienation, giving it more publicity than even its own assiduous public relations deserved and justifying their own desertion by looking for Labour's beams and motes. The fringe of show business, art, cultural and entertainment figures, who had given glamour, excitement and attraction to Labour by attaching themselves to the party of progress, was trimmed by the desertions. The ornaments of Gaitskell's Labour Party were being hung round the brass neck of the SDP.

The result was to create a bourgeois block on Labour's road to power. The new support in the country came from all sections, though mainly the middle class. An ORC survey in November 1981 of 5,500 SDP members showed 57 per cent professional and managerial, 67 per cent who had not been members of another party, 33 per cent who had voted Labour last time, 32 per cent Liberal, 24 per cent Conservatives. The activists who poured in – 51,800 members in eight weeks – were often innocents but with certain prejudices, anti-union, pro-progress, providing it did not endanger their status or their perks such as mortgage tax relief. Asked what the SDP should be, 34 per cent plumped for 'a party of radical change', 65 per cent for 'a party of moderate reform'. Yet those who provided the backbone and the experience came from Labour's ranks. They had become increasingly disenchanted with Labour's new incarnation. If they did not have enough strength to change Labour they could stop it by becoming a barrier between it and power. The revenge of the bourgeoisie.

The liberated bourgeoisie threw themselves into a frenzy of policy formulation; a policy factory worthy of Bennery. But better. Freed from Labour's shackles and idées fixes they decimated sacred cows and developed an attractive wide range of policies centering on decentralisation, decency and democracy with a massive dose of proportional representation and a smaller one of Keynes. From too little policy they suddenly had far too much. It was undoubtedly fun. Yet their basic role was more dubious. They spoke the language of idealism, of easing the shackles of dead dreams, breaking the mould of politics. They were in fact engaged in a political confidence trick. No third party can break through overnight unless the majority party splits. Labour, particularly faced with its new challenger, was not going to split. Some of the defectors assured those who remained on the right that they went ahead to prepare a bolt-hole, a hostel for battered and unreselected MPs. Yet in fact the split only underlined the importance of keeping Labour together and indirectly strengthened the right in the party, increasing its power to tilt the new party balance their way. So when Labour's house of cards refused to collapse the new activists had to carry out a confidence trick, creating an impression of unstoppable momentum to build up the idea that this would push the SDP through the barriers to majority status, dynamics doing what division could not. In fact this was impossible. There was a widespread alienation from the two party system, the surge in SDP voting showed that. Yet realistically it was bound to be a minority phenomenon. Lifelong allegiances do not disappear overnight. Labour was certain to maintain enough strength in the unions and in its heartlands to remain the largest single party in opposition and hence dominant in the House. They could harm Labour but not eclipse it. So in going for breakthrough the SDP was deceiving the people and peddling a confidence trick. They were middle class wreckers behaving rather like Trotskyites for the only logic to their approach was that things had to be made worse before they could be made better: the opposition had to be destroyed, the two party system smashed, a change in the electoral system forced, then Britain would at last be free to get on with the job of providing a better yesterday. However the mood was right, people were fed up with the major parties, and by-elections offer opportunities which general elections do not. So the dynamic was developed, the freshness merchandised in a promotion worthy of TV AM and as devoid of substance. The most attractive wares (plus some Pitts) were put on show at a series of by-elections: strong Labour Warrington in June, marginal Croydon in October, and strong Tory Crosby in November. The technique was simple: create an impression of momentum, an unstoppable bandwaggon which would attract votes predominantly from the under-party in the constituency, jumping on to get their opponents out. In Warrington 29 per cent of the 1979 Labour vote went to the SDP, 60 per cent of the Conservative vote. In Croydon the percentages were 31 per cent and 32 per cent, in Crosby 62 per cent and 35 per cent as Labour collapsed.

Two out of three by-elections, a lead in the polls and 70,000 members in less than a year was a rocket-assisted take-off. It could not be sustained. Next year membership fell off and the haggling with the Liberals over the share-out of seats was followed by the almost metaphysical definition process of their relationship and which was superior. All this produced a set-back in both polls and prospects. Despite the decline Hillhead was won by Roy Jenkins, a week before the Falklands war began, though now with only a third of the vote. Finally the Falklands factor hammered the loss home. The bubble had burst much earlier than in the Heath period. Yet the SDP, united with the Liberals and Alliance, had still taken the third party vote over the Liberal heights of 1973. Britain had acquired not a three-party but a 2.5-party system overnight.

Hot heads in the Labour Party responded with bitterness and glad cries of 'good riddance to bad rubbish'. In fact desertion harmed both Labour and the deserters. They were marching into the wasteland with only hopes of a public relations miracle to sustain them. Worse, it harmed the electorate. As depression got worse and it became clearer that government economic policies were not going to work, the possibility of securing acceptance for any alternative was undermined. It is the job of opposition to generate, propagate and polarise alternatives. It sells them on the basis of its own reputation and credibility to an electorate unable to understand the economics involved but ready to accept policies on trust as part of a package of change. Now the clear alternative was turned into a confused babble of voices, just at the moment when the electorate was least equipped to follow what was going on. The only possible lever for democratic change, the two-party system itself, was deadlocked. Discontent was syphoned away from the Labour alternative, creating the possibility of a split in the anti-Tory vote like that of the 1920s and 1930s which had entrenched Tory governments in power. Within less than a year Labour's hopes had been transformed. What looked to be a certainty of power, being ahead in polls with most electors expecting that Labour would win the election, had declined to being third in a three-party race. The only possibility of victory was beginning to look as if it were through one of those perverse tricks which the first-past-the-post electoral system is capable of when three parties run fairly close to each other. To be slightly ahead of the third party in such a situation was the difference between survival and humiliation. To be ahead of the pack was very heaven. Few realists in the Labour ranks could have had any reason for hoping for that.

5 · Confronting the Icebergs

If at Brighton the Labour Party and the trade unions allow the Tory press to pick our leadership, Fleet Street will write our next manifesto, choose our next cabinet and dictate the policy of the next Labour government.

TONY BENN

Purify the party, project the policies were the basis of new modelling hopes for the victory. That vision had great appeal to those who saw the party as a crusade, to paranoiacs who saw politics as a struggle against overwhelming odds and to the great communicator, Tony Benn, educator of his people. Unfortunately Labour lived in a different world. Those tinged with Marx see politics as struggle; those who look to the sweaty reality of voters see it as a calculus. Activists look to activity, particularly those old-fashioned forms which comfort impotence: marches, demonstrations, pickets, all things they can organise in their DIY way. Party managers look to the new media, persuading and cajoling, coaxing, not bullying or alarming, the bland leading the blind. Enthusiasts look to the only section they really understand, people like themselves. Realists look to broad, simple appeals to maximise support. The ideologue expects victory. He is right. The strategist sees himself as righter than the other lot but accepts that proving it means working, begging, pleading and cajoling. Even deceit and deviousness can be as relevant as bright burning principles. It's all a question of psychology.

The electorate itself was in transition, as always. In the heyday of the two-party system, the immediate post-war period, early British voting studies came as a shock to those who believed in rational politics. The electorate looked like two massive armies facing each other in mutual incomprehension across the party lines. The membership of each side was largely determined by allegiances inherited from parents and reinforced by background, neighbourhood, place of work and life-style, a broad working- or middle-class identification in a class-divided society which implied a rooted and permanent allegiance to Labour or the Conservatives. Floating voters, those rare creatures who crossed the party lines, emerged as somehow unworthy – their allegiances, their interest and even their information weaker than those of the 'constant' voters, who tramped to the polls at each election on automatic pilot, voting for the same party almost as a conditioned reflex, showing dissatisfaction by not bothering rather than changing sides. It was a picture of massive stability and slow, almost glacial change. The Butler-Stokes survey of the British electorate in the 1960s underlined this by emphasising the change in the electorate as cohort groups moved up; older electors with allegiances formed in the days of the three-party system died off, younger electors, growing up in the age when Labour had become a majority party, came along.

Yet things were already changing. The massive swings against incumbent governments and the more frequent changes of government in the era of uncertainty were outward and visible signs of a more volatile electorate. Polls showed it first, then the academic studies, such as Hilde Himmelweit's long-term panel, and the Essex University studies. Change was becoming the dominant pattern. Both blocks and allegiances were becoming weaker and looser. If two-fifths of the electors had been Labour and two-fifths Tory immediately post-war, by the 1970s these blocks were under a third, by the 1980s perhaps a quarter, and the attachment to their respective parties was cooler. A fifth of the electorate classified itself as 'very strong Conservative', a fifth 'very strong Labour' in 1964. By 1979 this was down to a tenth each. Taken together blocks were still a majority of the electorate. But only just, and the old technique of 'getting out the vote' had to be changed for a new and more difficult art: using the committed vote as the foundation stone of a bigger edifice, a coalition.

Erosion was the inevitable result of social change, the destruction of neighbourhoods and industries, the complexity of society and its multifarious skills, the increasing uniformity of consumer affluence and the life-style it imposed. Self-sustaining attitudes were eroded by the new media; politics and television exposed everyone to other parties, other arguments. The increasing inability of either party in power to deliver the rising standard of living the people had come to expect weakened loyalties, encouraged alienation. Both parties failed the major test of instrumentality and benefit. Ivor Crewe drew attention to this erosion of the blocks. On his interpretation the trends worked mainly against Labour, a party he in fact had deserted for the SDP, advising the Gang of Four early on that their day had come. There was a wider gulf between Labour policies, particularly nationalisation, equality and the ideological policies and the attitudes of Labour supporters. The ethos and ethics of the consumer society were at variance with those Labour preached, speaking in ideological terms to an unideological and increasingly unresponsive electorate. Tories, on the other hand, moved with the times and preached a new populism. Heath spoke it at Selsdon and for his first eighteen months in office. Margaret Thatcher spoke more volubly: anti-monolith, pro-tax-cutting, anti-bureaucrat, anti-scrounger. She went on to put it all into practice as near, and it was not very close, as could be done, capitalising on the frustrations of the new society which Labour had ignored.

An electorate whose allegiances were weaker and more uncertain was increasingly open to influence by the media. They viewed the world through blue-tinged glasses. The popular press was overwhelmingly Tory by ownership and instinct. Its main bond with its audience was to take popular prejudices, amplify them and relay them back to the people, thus making them respectable. Television tended to interpret its nominal impartiality by following the cues from the press or merely putting MPs on to balance each other out, thus propagating the image of politics as wrangling, strengthening alienation, not sense. The attitudes, assumptions and personnel of the electronic media were all overwhelmingly middle-class. It fought shy of explaining, because to do so was to take a point of view, but it was adept at the negative arts of destruction, harassing and questioning. The facts it poured out were never fitted into any framework of interpretation or even attitudes. Its whole achievement was negative, pouring out factoids to back Tory populism, not Labour positivism.

Labour ran the electoral race with a ball and chain fixed round its left leg. Yet proponents of the block erosion theory were wrong to give the impression that the process doomed Labour. If the electorate was anomic, increasingly volatile and footloose, responding to stimuli rather than rooted to old allegiances, then it was also up for grabs. It could still be won, it was just more difficult. If the blocks were eroding, this was happening on both sides. If allegiances were looser, it merely meant bigger swings against both governments in power and a more dramatic response to events, such as the ritual suicide of Ted Heath's Tory government, or Labour's suttee on the pyre of incomes policy in 1979. It was certainly not a one-horse race.

The clearest indication came immediately after the full exposition of the argument that Labour was locked into a spiral of decline. Margaret Thatcher promptly enjoyed the shortest honeymoon of any modern British prime minister. Labour moved ahead in the polls in August 1979 and stayed there, less than half a dozen points ahead in 1979, twice that in 1980. Then the party led every month and ended 1980 with a 50 per cent share, sixteen points ahead. Not bad for a party whose obituary had been so frequently written. The real problem was not so much Labour's unique unattractiveness as the ability of modern British governments to lose votes. Labour had been so much in power that government unpopularity had reflected adversely on it. From 1979 it began to benefit.

Until the tide turned. It was at this point that experience under Thatcherism began to diverge from the precedent of the Health administration. Labour had then gone into the lead after eight months but had stayed there through 1971, 1972 and 1973 with the exception of transient blips in April 1972 and December 1973. Now things went wrong earlier, not because Conservative support rose as it had on those two earlier dates but because the Labour vote slumped from its high of 50 per cent in October 1980 to a crippling low of 27 per cent by November 1981 at the alliance peak. It was no coincidence that in those twelve months Labour behaved in a fashion which exacerbated all the underlying problems it faced with the new electorate. Instead of working with the grain, reaching out and appealing to the volatile electorate, it concentrated on its internal preoccupations, acting as if all that was necessary was to rally the faithful. This put the party out of kilter with the new electorate. It was a decision not to win over but to confront the electorate. The slogan was, 'Don't let the media dictate policy' but the reality was 'Don't listen to the people. Tell them what the party thinks'.

The electorate is instinctively conservative, preferring what it regards, or can be persuaded to regard, as 'sound' men. Gallup regularly asked people if they saw themselves as left or right. Around a quarter (23 per cent at the end of 1979, 25 per cent at the same stage of 1982) said 'left' and only four per cent 'far' or 'substantially' left. Almost half (44 per cent and 50 per cent at the same dates) said 'right', a tenth 'middle'. At each stage between six out of ten and two-thirds saw Labour as 'left' and a proportion, increasing from a quarter to a third, as 'far' or 'substantially left'. The party which had undergone a genuine extremist takeover, the Tories, were also seen as pretty extreme, with nearly half describing them as 'substantially' or 'far' right but that was a crime which mattered less to the conservative nation.

The electorate's fears are readily excited by the media. Yet Labour was proudly presenting itself as daring, left, socialist and effectively, though more unconsciously, as irresponsible. The image that Labour was too much to the left was made worse by the increasing argument about permeation from the left. Here Labour got the worst of all worlds first by supressing the Underhill enquiry into the Militant Tendency, then by the controversy provoked when the right-wing protested and finally by passing by a huge conference majority a resolution in favour of a register, then finding itself unable to do more that expel the few leading members of *Militant*. Rather like Brer Rabbit and the tar baby, Labour could neither accept nor eliminate the mess. Maximum discredit, minimum effect was again the result.

Enthusiasts vote on policy lines. Others have a broad general impression of a party, a managerial assessment. There is the expectation that a party will look and act like a united body, able and competent to carry through its programmes, ready to step into power and run the country. Labour in opposition has always found it more difficult to present such an image than the Tories. The Conservative Party in power has been incompetent and lost votes. In opposition it has concentrated on policies with a broad appeal, in inverse ratio to a practicality which usually proved ruinous later. Labour is the opposite – divided and argumentative in opposition, because it is thrashing out its policies, more respectable in power because clothed with the mantles of office and responsibility.

The reforms were acceptable. A poll by NOP in August 1980 showed a majority against MPs electing their leader or Labour MPs controlling the manifesto and a large majority for re-selection. The problem was not the reforms but the rows that went with them. Now that weakness was heightened by the bitterness of the internal struggle. 'Is Labour united or divided?' the polls asked the public. The Conservative Party, with its struggle of dry rot against rising damp, was reported as united by over two-thirds. Labour, already torn in 1979, thanks to the activity of the NEC was then reported as divided by three-quarters, united by 16 per cent. By 1982 less than a tenth talked of unity, nine out of ten of division. In opposition Tories concentrate on generalities and intentions. With the depression offering great scope, Labour concentrated on constitutional issues, techniques, cataloguing the minutiae of method and venturing into realms certain to be alarming and unpopular. The public judge on an impression of competence which a party arguing bitterly finds it difficult to project. The government could do so even though its policies were disastrously wrong for it was judged on manner, not substance, particularly after the Falklands imbroglio proved folly, courage and determination to be military virtues. The government deftly fastened on the Resolute Approach to indicate that they were interchangeable with the economic sphere. Labour, divided, obviously disliking each other, headed by a leader who was clearly as good at economics as Sir Alec Douglas Home, never projected the same image of competence.

Michael Foot's was an image of incompetence and irrelevance. His age and woolliness enforced it. The main way of reaching the people was through television. Michael Foot preferred the meeting and the demonstration. The public wanted to be given confidence in the party. He could not project it. The party needed firm leadership. It was not forthcoming. His poll rating began bad and got worse, lagging more than twenty percentage points behind his rival. Such a leader could never drag Labour out of popularity doldrums. Unfortunately soon after his accession the party began to plunge. By the end of 1981 Labour's lead had vanished. Before the Falklands invasion the party had got back to neck and neck but at only a third of the electorate each. As soon as General Galtieri intervened on Mrs Thatcher's behalf the Conservatives romped ahead – as any government must in a national crisis.

Experience diverged from that of 1970–74. Then the third party had never outstripped either of the other two. Its highest point, August 1973, had been only a quarter of the electorate. From October 1981 to February 1982 it was ahead of both, its peak coinciding with the peak of interest and mortgage rates. In the early 1970s Labour had been ahead, so the Tories with a softer vote were clearly more threatened by the Liberals who were in any case more readily acceptable as an alternative conservative party. Now Labour was on the downslide. 'Do you think most people are holding a favourable opinion of the Labour Party?' Gallup polled. Yes, said over one third of the samples in 1979 and 1980, just under half said no. By 1982 the yesses were less than a quarter and for three months under a fifth, the noes well over two-thirds. Those feelings persisted into 1983. Labour looked a mess. So its vote was far softer than it had been under Heath, particularly since his crisis, the miners' strike, was on Labour's strong suit, Thatcher's was on war, Labour's weakness. Those who blithely assumed that the Alliance would merely syphon off Tory malcontents had little idea of the political realities or of the way in which third parties threaten limping competitors whether in government or in opposition.

Table 1 *Are you satisfied or dissatisfied with the way*
Mrs Thatcher is doing her job as prime minister?
Mr Foot is doing his job as leader of the opposition?

| | THATCHER | | CALLAGHAN/FOOT | |
	satisfied %	*dissatisfied %*	*satisfied %*	*dissatisfied %*
1979				
3rd Q	42.5	48	45.5	33
1980				
1st Q	37.6	53.6	39	39
2nd Q	42.5	51	39	40
3rd Q	36.6	57	40	42
4th Q	33	59.5	23	21
1981				
1st Q	31.3	63	23.6	44
2nd Q	33.5	60.5	26.5	48.5
3rd Q	29.3	63.6	24.6	50.3
4th Q	27.6	65	18.6	61
1982				
1st Q	32.6	60.3	20	60.3
2nd Q	52	43	18.6	63.6
3rd Q	48.6	44	14.3	67.6
4th Q	46.8	45.6	21.4	60
1983				
1st Q	48	45.3	18.3	65

Though the Church of England was rapidly becoming the
SDP at prayer, God himself remained as devout a Tory as
ever, giving Mrs Thatcher far more than fair chances. Just as
Labour began to appreciate the scale of the disaster it had
inflicted on itself, and the Alliance bubble began to deflate,
down thirteen points in three months, early in 1982 came the
Falkland crisis. This was inevitably a no-win situation for the
opposition, and particularly a Labour opposition, a bonus for
the government, particularly one led by an actress looking
for a role. The government's vote surged thirteen points in
two months.

Michael Foot's leadership in the Falklands crisis was

Table 2 *Do you think most people are
holding a favourable opinion of the Labour Party?*

	Conservative %	Labour %	Liberal/SDP combined %	Conservative lead %
1979				
4th Q	40.5	45.5	12	−5
1980				
1st Q	38.6	45	13.6	−6.3
2nd Q	40	43.5	13.5	−3.5
3rd Q	37	47	13.6	−6
4th Q	35	50	14	−15
1981				
1st Q	32	41.3	24.6*	−9.3
2nd Q	30.5	38.5	28	−7
3rd Q	29	37.6	31	−8.6
4th Q	27	29	43.5†	−2
1982				
1st Q	31	32.3	34.6	−1.3
2nd Q	42.3	29.3	27	+13
3rd Q	43.6	30.6	24.3	+13.3
4th Q	42.4	33.6	22.2	+8.8
1983				
1st Q	43.8	31.6	23.1	+11.6

* SDP formed.
† Alliance formed.

honest and honourable, cleaving firmly to the path of negotiation. From him it looked inadequate. Mrs Thatcher's combination of irresponsibility and blood and guts looked like
courage in the Lilliputian war against bankrupt incompetence which is all modern Britain can manage. Yet his failure
was not the test of war, it was a general failure to lead. At
his best on the Falklands, where he was beaten, he launched
no convincing, powerful onslaught on the government in the
House of Commons, where his party was desperate for him
to succeed. He gave no solace to a public groping for an
alternative. He ignored the wider audience to talk to the
Labour Party. Even there he led it in no particular direction,

for the habits of a lifetime made him all things to all men, but more of them to the left, fudging decisions, going to visit EEC socialist leaders and listening to their highly publicised criticisms of Labour's EEC policy, but making no effective reply except to give the impression that he was a two-way bearer of bad news, not a decisive influence. When he needed backing by an able dynamic team, he let shadow cabinet meetings ramble on with no lead, no positive impetus. In his appointments he brought in chums from the Tribune group but little lively new blood. The Labour front bench presented as tired and weak an appearance as a government five years in power. A party which per acre had far more ability than the Conservatives thus projected the image of inadequacy, while the government, a dominant woman surrounded by minions, projected ability.

Michael Foot's greatest achievement was to hold together a party which at times appeared to be in danger of falling apart. That was what he had been elected for, a job he did well. He did not try particularly hard or effectively to hold the SDP but that might have been impossible. He had certainly done his best to prevent the Bennite follies of 1981 and to project a concept of the party to which all but the most revolutionary could rally. He had pushed the party towards policy, the one area in which solace could be found by working together for a finite objective. He had cooled the fever.

All this was a real achievement, received with gratitude by both left and right. Yet it implied a process of accommodation with the left. A fight could have yielded the same benefits as Gaitskell's 'fight, fight and fight again' but such clear-cut ground was not available. In being forced to concentrate on the party Michael Foot was fulfilling only one of two responsibilities a Labour leader has. He must manage the party internally, lead it forward in enthusiasm and unity, something which requires a feeling of impetus; stalled parties get bored and fractious. He must also appeal to the wider electorate which must be won for Labour. The second role had traditionally been the most important. The more effective of the other eleven leaders, MacDonald, Attlee, Gaitskell, Wilson, Callaghan, had all appealed to the wider public.

Michael Foot concentrated enthusiastically, almost

unremittingly, on the first. He had no alternative. Helped by the fear produced by the Benn bandwagon, he did it. Yet it was also the only role he was happy with. His contribution on the other was mainly in the field of demonstrations, meetings and rallies, which appealed to party members but hardly at all outside, maintaining the image of Labour as the party of permanent demonstration with unruly, chanting mobs, led by a limping figure with a walking stick. That the internal role absorbed him so completely was a sympton of the party's weakness as well as a cause.

The leader is a prisoner of his time. When the mood is favourable to Labour it is difficult for a leader to put a foot wrong. When the tide runs the other way he collects the blame and in the situation to which Labour had reduced itself, more powerful leadership was impossible. That was the conclusion to which the party itself had come and Michael Foot had therefore been appropriately chosen. Yet real competence, an impression of dynamism, could have distracted attention from the problems. Instead Michael Foot had an amazing capacity for tripping himself up. He was pressed, by the northern group of MPs and the threat of resignation from Bob Mellish, to disown Peter Tatchell's Bermondsey candidacy as an embarrassment to the party, certain to precipitate a by-election and endanger a seat which it was then thought Shirley Williams must capture. Peter Tatchell, though not himself a *Militant*, the spokesman of *Militants*, became a symbol for all the headbanger candidates local parties were selecting, occasionally in winnable seats, as demonstrations of their ideological purity. As the more exposed he had to be made an example for the others. Michael Foot concurred and chose the most public possible forum to demonstrate the fact. In prime minister's question time he announced that Tatchell 'is not and as long as I am leader will not be an endorsed member of the Labour Party.' The fact that this was later altered to 'candidate' caused some charitably to assert that Michael Foot had misheard Tatchell for Tariq Ali, then trying to enter the party. The explanation will not hold. Foot had been told the day before of Jim Wellbeloved's generous intention to turn the knife in the Bermondsey wound in a parliamentary question. The condemnation was considered; a weak man's response to a bad situation. Attempting to show himself stronger than he was able to be, he had the choice of carrying out his proclaimed intention and risking humiliation on the National Executive or climbing down and facing public humiliation. The first would have been the honourable course. The second he chose. Tatchell was allowed to stand for the new selection and predictably, because the Bermondsey Party was still crazy after all these months, he was again selected. Instead of fighting either decision and throwing his weight, that of his inveterate supporters John Evans and Neil Kinnock, and his prestige, which counted for less, into the scales, Foot discerned a total change in Tatchell's attitude, and shook hands with him outside the House of Commons, in a photo opportunity too good for the press to miss. He ignored the possibility of selecting candidates to win seats for Labour rather than gestures of defiance. Yet a posturing Australian who was pilloried by the press as a homosexual and a draft dodger did not seem overwhelmingly attractive to an aging, working-class Catholic constituency for other reasons than his arcane views on extra-parliamentary action.

Foot had set both himself and the party up for public humiliation. The press duly obliged, using its front pages to talk to the electors of Bermondsey and to caricature Tatchell, none too difficult a process. They were followed by television, seeing the press campaign as sanction for their own crudities, not a reason to redress the balance. It was a campaign of the type which the Alliance had made classic, pushing off a bandwagon against the leading candidate and then jumping on it. This time the press had its shoulders behind the wheel. By using polls, particularly telephone polls with a built-in bias against Labour and in favour of the Alliance, the press gave the public the kind of information the French national electorate has in its second ballots: who was ahead and what to do to block. Bermondsey took advantage of it to reject one exotic character with a 38 per cent fall in the Labour vote and elect the only man who could beat him, an Englishman who was a better self-publicist but on traditional lines. Foot and the Labour Party, after a brief rise to 35 per

cent in late 1982, fell back to 27 per cent in March 1983. The
Alliance revived and moved ahead.

Labour was unlikely to win an early election. It stood no
chance under Michael Foot. A party absolutely clear about
its responsibilities to the nation, and particularly to the
unemployed section of it could, and should, have responded
accordingly. The effectiveness of change was dramatically
indicated in New Zealand where the death, in the Great
Depression, of an old, unpopular and doctrinaire leader of
the Labour Party had created an explosion of emotion
cleverly exploited by a protracted funeral which had helped
carry Labour in power in 1935. It was difficult to argue that
British Labour needed a good funeral so another example
was better. In Australia Bill Hayden, though no Michael
Foot, a perfectly competent leader in fact, was replaced
when the election was announced by Bob Hawke, a charis-
matic and popular figure who fought the election campaign
without policy commitments of any kind. Labour, which had
seemed certain of defeat when Malcolm Fraser called his
early election, romped home to victory.

The lesson was not lost in the British party. A group of
young Turks, rising young front-benchers such as Jack Straw,
Jeff Rooker, who had voted for Foot and regretted it, and
Phillip Whitehead, who hadn't but regretted that others had,
began to meet and air their own discontents to the press,
non-attributably. Dale Campbell-Savours, faced with a
chorus of constituency complaint about Michael Foot, raised
the matter bluntly in the PLP meeting but was supported
only by Barry Sheerman. Only Walter Johnson spoke publicly and he was not of the same stature. All this was inevitably highly publicised, as if some effective plot was afoot. It
wasn't. Channel Four polled nearly half the Labour MPs and
found nearly a quarter saying the party was unlikely to win
with Michael, two-fifths thinking Denis as leader would
improve its chances. Dale Campbell-Savours, incensed at the
party's betrayal of people who looked to it, if it didn't go all
out to win, began to poll, interviewing 117 MPs, mostly on
the left, and found ninety-six saying unequivocally that
Michael Foot should go, including some of the most surpris-
ing people on the left actually wanting Healey as leader.

Others, too, were polling. West Midlands MPs were reported to think Foot should go but not every sounding was as clear-cut. Most people were waiting on by-election events. The only concrete result was a few individual decisions, notably Jeff Rooker's to go to the leader to tell him he should retire.

The stirrings were treated as if they constituted a major threat by Michael's protectors, particularly Stans Orme and Newens who organised a Save Michael counter-action while his PPS, John Evans, went round nipping discontent in the bud. Unions such as the EEPTU, AEUW and COHSE rallied round. The party office-holders, who should have been relaying back the real state of opinion, acted instead to protect the leader. Michael Cocks and the whips' office were urged to carry out an official sounding on the state of opinion in the party. Cocks, who repented his own vote for Foot in 1980, declined, on the grounds that news of it would leak out and destroy confidence in the credibility of the leader. A wise thought. That was the intention. The whips' office was divided but majority opinion was against a sounding. Others, including the young Turks, continued their own soundings. Most thought Michael Foot a liability. Yet most also thought it too late for change and too difficult to carry it out while the Scots, assured of winning, were less interested in a change. Had it been easy, straightforward and with a guarantee that there would be no contest, it would have been overwhelmingly popular, but neither the new structure nor the ever uncertain propensities of Tony Benn could offer any guarantee of that. Jack Dormand, the chairman of the PLP, though asked to relay requests that Foot should go, did not do so. Dormand, a canny lad, considered from his own knowledge of the mood of the party that such views were minority mutterings. In his view, the bulk of the party wanted Foot to stay. Denis Healey, approached by some of the malcontents, took a strictly honourable line. He was deputy, would work loyally with Michael, could not and would not have anything to do with moves against him. Healey was the only possibility for a clean, automatic succession, taking over as leader until the next conference which could not be before October. He would not have been challenged by Roy Hattersley and probably not by Peter Shore, though no one could assay Tony Benn. Thus Healey's honour sustained a man he could easily have outclassed as leader.

No one was prepared to approach the leader and tell him he had no clothes. I had screwed up the nerve to go, first with another marginal seat member, then, when he dropped out, on my own. At that point my book, *The Case for Labour*, was published. Michael, ever the most intellectually interested and considerate of the shadow cabinet, was the only member to come to the launch. I gave up my contemplated brutality. It would have done no good in any case. The only people the leader would have listened to were those he trusted, those who had voted for him in the first place, better still those he relied on: Orme or Booth to whom such a proposal was unthinkable, Norman Buchan who understood the situation but opposed the proposal, or perhaps Neil Kinnock who was devoted to him. But Kinnock took refuge in the Footite strategy of hoping that 1983 would go away.

The real barrier to change was the difficulty of carrying it through. Had the parliamentary party retained power it would have been possible to find a Brutus in shadow cabinet: some had already relayed their feelings directly. Less likely was a move in the parliamentary party. The PLP has become a public forum. Hence real power has left it. Power now lay with the electoral college, so cumbersome, so discrediting in its operations, that no one dare use it. The college protected a leader who had failed. So did the lack of a guiding elite in the party. Labour had no magic circle like the Tory Party of old when Salisbury, Devonshire and the chief whip might have been able to take a leader by the arm and say, 'Enough is enough.' Now those days were gone in the Tory Party, and Devonshire to the SDP. They had never existed in the Labour Party and the local equivalent of the Knights of the Shire, the trade union group, remained loyal to Michael. So it was in the interests of all that Michael Foot should go, but in no one's interest specifically. A lot of wishful thinking was directed to the unions: 'The big boys will fix it.' They were incapable of doing so. The trade union leaders were desperate for Labour to win. Few saw any realistic hope of winning with Michael. Yet their collective characteristic is loyalty and all had different views. David Basnett agonised, Clive Jenkins was loyal, Moss Evans waffled and Terry Duffy and the EEPTU protected Michael. Thus the approaches which were made to trade unions got nowhere. There was no will to act but a collective propensity to wishful thinking.

Bermondsey was Michael Foot's nadir. On *Weekend World* he compared the press campaign to get rid of him with the one which had got rid of Attlee and brought in Gaitskell, who had promptly lost the next election. He went on, 'It is my firm intention to carry out what I was elected to do . . . leaders of the Labour Party are not elected by polls or newspapers or by campaigns of this nature, they're elected by the process we'd agreed . . . I have an obligation to the people who voted for me in those elections apart from anything else and that's what I intend to carry out . . . indeed many of them have been coming forward in the past week or two expressing their will or desire that I should continue to fulfil that . . . a long list. There are other people take a different view. Not so many of them have been prepared to come forward and say it but . . . the proper way for them to do it under the Labour Party arrangements is to put up a candidate . . . I was elected for the purpose of trying to unite the party in preparation for the next election, I believe the overwhelming majority of the party, in parliament, in the country, in the trade unions, want me to do that.'

The fight back was less important than the strategy: to make the Darlington by-election an immediate test. Darlington was the counter-coup. Even before the Bermondsey result, Michael Cocks and Foot's friend, Jim Mortimer, the general secretary, persuaded the leader to call the Darlington by-election three weeks after Bermondsey and against the advice of the local organiser who wanted it delayed. The haste was indecent. The hope was that the success in a seat much more likely to be favourable to Labour, up in the real world, and with a much better candidate than so many others, could redeem the situation. It was a high risk strategy but it protected the leader. Dale Campell-Savours was persuaded not to oppose the moving of the by-election writ which he had intended to do on the grounds that it was only being done to protect a leader who should go. Jim Mortimer announced, 'We have a particular strength in Michael Foot.' Discontent was temporarily silenced. There remained only muttered hopes that Michael might seize a victory to go with honour and wishes, never expressed, that Labour might lose and decide the matter for him. That was not what was being planned.

Darlington was not won, the Alliance candidate threw it away. Yet the campaign cheered everyone. The seat was held with a swing of 1.6 per cent to Labour, the Bermondsey rot was stopped, and Labour heaved a sigh of relief at what in normal circumstances should have been interpreted as a poor election augury. Michael Foot could stay on. Dale Campbell-Savours put his list away, deciding that the time was not ripe. The muttering and the soundings stopped. Labour had decided to hope for the best, an indication of how low the party's sights had sunk. Ossie O'Brien entered his short career as a parliamentarian, receiving a particularly warm welcome from Michael Foot whose leadership he had saved. The crisis was over. Michael Foot's determination was rewarded – in much the same way as Margaret Thatcher's was in the economic sphere.

As usual Michael Foot was little considered in all the to-ing and fro-ing. Yet he had no intention of going. Largely unaware of the nagging doubts and discontents within the party, buoyed up by hope and his wife, seeing his duty to lead the party to socialism and to initiate the British nuclear disarmament, he was determined not to go. There is a tide in the affairs of leaders. Which Labour's missed.

The shape in which Labour was to fight the election was determined. It was also one of the major reasons why the government decided to go early. Since 1981 Labour had drawn back from the brink. It was coming together not so much because Tony Benn's political activity seemed to have reduced itself to frequent pleas for unity, as because so many were aghast at what had happened. Party members and candidates all over the country were discovering that the gulfs between them were not what they had supposed. They had mainly been fighting stereotypes and trading labels, rather than dealing with fundamental realities. The 1982 conference was a pleasant change after its three disastrous predecessors. Moreover there is a law of party dynamics. Divisions widen after election defeat. There is a surge left, then a drawing together and finally a shift to the right as the election approaches. This is not calculation but inevitability.

That process occurred now but from too low a starting point and too late. The shift to a wholly new concept of the party had gone too far for the drawing back to be more than cosmetic. It was in any case all in vain for the two fundamental problems were not tackled. The leadership was not changed. Though there was loyalty to Michael and gratitude for lancing the Benn boil, no one with any clear-eyed perception of reality could have thought that Labour could win under him. This undermined morale and compounded the problems. Nor had the policy problem been tackled. Nothing was done before the election announcement. There was no time to do anything after it, though on the day one shadow cabinet member asked Michael to step down.

Thus a party just back from the gates of hell with the smell of sulphur still impregnating its clothes prepared, or rather did not prepare, to meet its maker. The enthusiastic had assumed that the scale of the Thatcher disaster and the rise in unemployment must radicalise the people. Even those who did not like the two-party alternation tended to assume fair do's would be done and it must be Labour's turn next. The optimism was baseless. The Great Depression, though not producing a job loss as great as Margaret Thatcher's, had not radicalised but had in fact decimated Labour and entrenched a Tory government in power for over a decade. Unemployment generates not altuism but fear, driving those who suffer from it home to close the door on their misery and driving the rest apart from them, determined to hang on to the advantage they have. It breaks the power of the unions by making people afraid for their jobs. It weakens the attraction of change and daring solutions. It makes people cling to what they know.

The British people were living in a fool's misery. Things were bad, people were worried. Yet they half believed the government's confident assertion that there was no alternative for they did not understand what had gone wrong nor what could be done about it. Their knowledge of economics was such that they were prone to think courage and sacrifice were economic policies in themselves. Oil was the key to their inertia. Britain's decline, which would have been cataclysmic in terms of job loss, cuts in living standards, collapse of the nation's ability to pay its way, was heavily cushioned by oil wealth. A balance of payments benefit of £14 billion a year allowed industry to decline but imports to be paid for. The tax benefits, £20 billion in government revenue since the Conservatives had come in, lightened a burden of taxation which would have been intolerable with each person out of work costing £5,000 in lost revenues and benefits paid out, because it was pressing on a shrinking productive base. North Sea oil was the solace and the only reason why the extent of the damage the government had done was not brought home to the people.

Government, ever solicitous for the comfort and well-being of its electors, also took steps to conceal reality, distorting it by a process of Goebellisation of the truth. This first entered British political life on any scale outside *Campaign Handbooks* because of the need to justify a Common Market which had always been a doubtful proposition economically but which had still to be sold to public opinion on those grounds because its political benefits were so well concealed. Proving it was working to Britain's benefit when it wasn't meant a propagandist's field day of fiddling figures to disguise a deficit in manufactured trade, currently running at £8 billion a year. These techniques now spilled into national policies as a government in difficulties sought to convince the people that all was well – or about to be so. Trade, it was argued, was booming when exports were down by 2 per cent on 1975, imports up 118 per cent. Productivity, it was said, was surging when it was going up less than the average under Labour and that only as a consequence of closures. Competitiveness, it was claimed, was improving when industry was being strangled by an overvalued pound and high interest rates, and was surviving only by jettisoning investment, training, research, design and development to keep afloat. There was a new realism, government said, when they meant a fear for jobs. Even the unemployment figures had been

Tebbitised by knocking 350,000 off the register. As for prosperity being just around the corner, recovery was a mirage.
It had already been cancelled in 1981 and 1982 and even now
was only the product of a deliberate conjuring trick. The
government's economic policy really reduced itself to one
simple argument which carried conviction because it
appeared logical. Britain's problems are due to inflation.
With that conquered, growth will come. There was no reason
why it should without the massive efforts other governments
were making to help it along. But the public half believed it.

Government also took the precaution of setting the scene
by a crude RAB Butler-style mini-boom. The relaxation of
hire purchase restrictions and a hefty run by the public on its
own savings cheered the High Streets and indicated that
video had a future as the opium of the people. Then, while
still priding itself on its financial discipline, government
relaxed it. It allowed a carefully concealed overshoot in
government spending. In the 1983 Public Expenditure White
Paper this was disguised by a series of fiddles such as cutting
the contingency reserve to the bone to allow other spending
to go up, and making dubious assumptions about inflation
and the effectiveness of cash and wage limits. Thus the economy could be superficially stimulated in a way which would
have to be cut short afterwards but which made things look
better for a time – an election time.

The government was also assiduously stealing Labour's
clothes. In 1982 Peter Shore unveiled Labour's plans for
expanding demand and stimulating the economy by a two-
stage devaluation. Government and its acolytes promptly fell
over themselves to distract attention from their own policies
by heaping ridicule on Labour's. The expansionary programme, it was claimed, would produce no boom but real
bust.

However, such proposals had attractions in the short term
so government, accidentally or deliberately, put them into
action. Demand was boosted by a huge expansion of domestic credit: £20 billion in the fifteen months up to 31 March
1983, treble the increase permitted by the Bank in the same
period before the 1979 election, double the increase in the
money supply, twice the increase in the level of transactions.

This huge boost, £10,000 billion net, and more than the increase actually proposed by Labour, was pumped out into the economy. The government was, in effect, printing money. Then from November 1982 the pound began to slip, down 14 per cent to the beginning of March, almost exactly the first stage of two devaluations proposed by Peter Shore in his illustrative computer run. Unlike the Shore devaluation this Thatcher (and therefore moral) one was unwanted. Yet the government found that industry was enjoying it. Economists and analysts who had been tireless in their advocacy of an overvalued pound quickly accommodated themselves to the advantage of a fall, which began to filter through in more competitive exports, less attractive imports and a greater optimism about prospects. So something the government had not only not wanted but had strenuously opposed as sin was found enjoyable. Its consequences were quickly commandeered by the government as the result of its own farsighted policies.

This propensity emerged despite the fact that government was assiduously undermining both developments. Given a decline in interest rates the expansion of demand could have passed into investment and hence growth. Interest rates had been lowered; it would have been amazing not to have lowered them as inflation fell if only to weaken the middle-class protest which had flowed to the SDP. Yet real interest rates remained high because inflation was low. So looser credit washed not into investment but into consumer demand and asset speculation – a 60 per cent rise in share prices over eighteen months. Mortgage credit was allowed to boom as funds for house-buying soared from £2,491 million in the fourth quarter of 1981 to £3,868 million in the same period of 1982 and higher still in the first quarter of 1983. Both boosted consumer demand. Spending asset gains was respectable Keynesianism. The result was an acceleration in house prices, always a stimulus to middle-class well being. None of this brought growth but it provided a feeling of buoyancy which was more useful to a government determined not to relax the discipline it had imposed on industry. Indeed government was seeking to reinforce that discipline by encouraging the pound back up. From the beginning of March sterling rose 10 per cent in real terms, mainly against the European currencies which are now Britain's main competition. The rise was sure to nip the promised recovery in the bud. But not yet. Thus the stage had been set for a happier electorate. 'Lighten our darkness,' they had implored in 1981, and Geoffrey Howe obliged in 1982, reinforcing the strategy of building a new Tory majority. While Labour hoped to make unemployment the dominant issue the government was defusing it by making everyone else better off. The standard of living of those in employment had risen since 1979. The national decline in living standards was wholly concentrated on the unemployed. An issue Labour was counting to turn the people against the government had also turned them against each other.

It was crucial to seize the moment before the City and the financial community began to clamour about the money supply, financial laxity and lack of respect for sound money. Action would then have to be taken to propitiate the gods. But again, not yet. The scenario for the 1983 election was clear. Government had set the stage while innocently disclaiming the idea of an early election and announcing that its duty was to carry on and see the nation through its problems. It worked. In January 22 per cent of the public said they expected economic conditions to improve, in February 26 per cent, in March 31 per cent, by April 36 per cent. The mood was right. Or righter.

Labour really wanted a 1984 election and half hoped it might get it. So it continued doing those things it ought not to have done and leaving undone those things it ought to have done. Everything possible had been done to lose the General Election in the thirty months which preceded it. In that time Labour dropped twenty points in the opinion polls by acquiring an unpopular and unrespected leader, and a reputation for disunity, extremism, crankiness and general unfitness to govern. It developed a profusion of policies in terms remote from the lives and hopes of millions of voters – including most of its own supporters – and rendered itself open to attack on basic issues of national defence, law and order, inflation, home ownership and individual freedom.

It now added to its problems by failing to develop an election strategy. The campaign committee did not meet until

November 1982 and then concerned itself primarily with organisational matters. The political leadership of the party was pre-occupied with drafting the (misnamed) Campaign Document so it never considered what basic issues and messages the Labour Party needed to present and never discussed either an advertising campaign or the content of its election broadcasts, or slogans, key statistics and punchlines for speeches. Within the party research department there appeared to be no special effort to divert resources to election-fighting. Indeed they decided *not* to prepare a campaign handbook for candidates on grounds of expense and the party's normal processses of 'policy development' spluttered on into the spring of 1983 with the preparation of an eighty-page document on the security services, an item occupying one obscure paragraph in the Campaign Document. The Campaign Document itself was a monument of misplaced effort: its preparation actually *prevented* the preparation of a popular manifesto and its convoluted style and content were in the end more use to the party's enemies than its supporters.

The nation waited, aware that Thatcherism wasn't working, but not sure why. The people knew they had not liked the last four years but were uncertain about an alternative, worried but beginning to think that moralising might be a strategy. The mood was well summed up by MORI's first opinion survey for Labour, a series of group discussions held all over the country with small groups specially selected to assess the attitudes of the electorate. Even that was belated but at last Labour was listening to the people. Three and a half years too late. The study itself should have been started in 1982 for in June 1982 Andrew Mackintosh – shortly to be a Labour peer as well as market researcher – proposed to Dick Clements that Labour commission a programme of market research beginning with a series of panel studies to listen to what the people were thinking and follow the changes starting in September. The study was costed and TULV would probably have made the money available to Michael Foot. Nothing happened until February 1983. Then the questions were hastily agreed by Walworth Road (even then with a fudge on the defence–nuclear disarmament issue) and the groups called together. The information MORI provided to Walworth Road staff to whom it reported was an invaluable indication of the mood of the electorate, had Labour been organised to use it and had its preparation not been delayed until immediately before the campaign. It reached the Campaign Committee like the voice of doom and dramatically summed up Labour's situation. And Britain's:

> The mood of the electorate as revealed by the group discussions was of helplessness and resignation in the face of the enormity of the problems facing the country. Cynicism about the political parties and lack of awareness of their policies combined to produce a feeling that the continuing decline in personal fortunes along with those of the country as a whole, was inevitable. Against such a background it was clear that many of this government's messages had struck a chord. A lot of potential Labour voters believed Mrs Thatcher's simple economic statements and the view that there was no alternative to the current strategy . . . . The general perception was that things would get worse before they improved – and this was as it should be because it was somehow morally right that we should atone for past sins . . . . Labour was perceived to be implausible as a party of government because it was disorganised, internally divided, pre-occupied with internal wrangling over policies, organisation and personalities, infiltrated by "communists" and out of touch with the voters . . . . It was also perceived to be shackled by the unions and to be old fashioned . . . . The leadership in general and Mr Foot in particular were widely perceived to be weak inconsistent, too old, and uninspiring despite being sincere and well meaning. The overall image was of a party in decline which was currently implausible as an alternative government. The image of the Conservatives was of a party which had set itself a long term strategy with determination. Although it had introduced some harsh measures many potential Labour voters believed they were necessary for the good of the country as a whole . . . . Although respondents expressed concern

about the high level of unemployment there was a feeling that the government was only partly to blame.
There was considerable uncertainty as to how Labour
proposed to tackle unemployment but unanimity that a
target of one million over five years was unrealis-
tic . . . . Respondents talked of the "ideal" party as one
which offered hope to the unemployed and school
leavers: did not engage in slanging matches, had policies which were relevant, actually did things rather than
simply talk about doing them, communicated in lay-
man's terms on its policies and how they would be
implemented, was united under strong clearly identified
leadership and worked for the good of the country.
Labour's image was far from that of the ideal party.

MORIturi te salutant.

6 · Disaster from the Jaws of Defeat

It is a possibility that the Labour Party will fail to win a majority at the next election. This would be mainly due to the vacillations and hesitations of the leadership of the Labour Party itself. With a firm will and socialist policies Labour could gain an overwhelming majority at the next election.

MILITANT

Oppositions don't win elections, governments lose. This conventional wisdom explains Harold Macmillan's 1959 survival in the autumn of affluence and 1979's fall in the winter of discontent. It applies to every previous post-war election but makes the implicit assumption that the opposition plays by the rules of the two-party game, presenting itself in a shape, and with policies and leadership calculated to win. Ready to take advantage of any fall from grace by the incumbents, it is ready to take over if government alienates support. This adage had little relevance to 1983. Government, despite all the superficial appearance of massive unemployment and a nation in decline, did nothing to accelerate its demise. Labour failed to do the same justice to itself.

The party was trapped. Its poll share drifted in the doldrums at just over 30 per cent, a third in the early part of the year, down for Bermondsey, up after it, yet never broke through a one-third barrier which was to become crucial. It was the least liked party. Gallup asked people if there was a party they did not want to win in their constituency and 40 per cent said 'Labour', 30 per cent 'Tory', 9 per cent 'Alliance'. The internal struggle was over, not because it had been decisively won, but because it had petered out: change could not be pushed any further, opponents could not roll it back and the deadlock could be called peace, allowing what had gone before it to be forgotten, as far as it could be, and permitting the party to begin its new task of 'putting over the policies' while waiting for the wounds to scar over, if not heal.

The government had more freedom of manoeuvre. It used it to the full. Margaret Thatcher likes to project an image as determined and long-sighted, the kind of woman ready to take tough measures and see them through. Yet she is also a brilliant quick-change artist, flitting from character to character, always acutely conscious of public relations. Every opportunist argument pointed to an early election. The economy had been carefully stage-managed and the opportunity it presented had to be seized before it vanished. The mood was more optimistic. In 1980 two-thirds of the public had been convinced that the economy would get worse. By early 1983 it was only a third, and the proportion thinking things would improve had more than doubled. Whatever happened to the real economy, the depression line falling and the optimism line rising had crossed. The government hit its highest level of support since 1979 with a good 17 per cent lead over Labour and, to Gallup's questions charting why people supported the Conservatives, the answers came clear and strong: Mrs Thatcher's strength of character, given by a third; the handling of the Falklands crisis, given by almost as many; the fall in inflation given by a quarter. Two of those reasons were certain to fade with time.

Realism pointed to an early election. The public were resigned to it. On 6 May 48 per cent told MORI that they preferred June, 15 per cent October, and 23 per cent 'next year'. Possibly too there was a calculation that the Tory Party might not have Michael Foot to kick around later. So everything pointed to early, not late. Alan Watkin's sudden announcement that 'Miss June Poll' was receding made it look absolutely certain.

The prime minister behaved with a political skill worthy of better causes. The election was unnecessary until June 1984, the last possible date for a parliament that had started life in May 1979. Nevertheless, early in 1983, she encouraged speculation about the possibility of an early election, leaked her own reluctance to seize advantage but at the same time boosted the speculation by Maggie-May coyness until it ran out of hand. She then stepped in to protect the country from speculation by announcing an election so early as to be almost indecent. On 8 May ministers went out to Chequers to discuss the situation. The prime minister told the 'World at One' that she had not yet made up her mind.The next day, with her press machine giving the impression she had decided over kippers, she went to the palace. The election was called for 9 June.

Labour was as well prepared as Poland in September 1939. All senior positions were held by men with no experience of running an election campaign: Michael Foot himself; Jim Mortimer, the general secretary, who had been recruited in 1982 from the union movement via ACAS; the national agent, David Hughes, who had been northern regional organiser in 1979; and Nick Grant, the press officer, who was only four months in the job, experienced as press officer for COHSE but lacking the press contacts and television experience his predecessors had had. The campaign committee made up in fullness of presence of shadows, NEC and officials, what was lacking in experience. It had already begun to meet and taken a few decisions, such as turning down a proposal for mass marches. It had not, however, applied itself to such major issues as where the press conferences were to be held, who was to do them, what the role of the leader and deputy leader was to be. Policy was half-baked. The Campaign Document had been taken out of the oven but common sense suggested boiling it down. The process of selecting candidates for the new constituencies, having been deliberately held up to make Labour's long and futile court action against the Boundary Commission look more justifiable, was two-thirds complete but a quarter of the 105 'key marginals' had no candidate. Some of the new parties for the new constituencies had not come into being.

Yet there was no shortage of money. Trade Unions for a Labour Victory had promised £2.5 million, half the Conservative spending and £1 million more than the Alliance total. Professional help was available on a scale not seen before. An advertising agency, John Wright and Partners,

had been selected and engaged. Picking an agency is a difficult business for the Labour Party. It does not know the field
and is not well organised or single-minded enough to be a
good client. It is also difficult for the agency which can face
pressure from clients and is certain to find Labour unfortunately opinionated and interfering. Wright's had two potential
clients pull out of discussions and one actual client expressed
doubts, speedily quashed. Yet the managing director was a
Labour supporter, it was the right size and enthusiastic, and
the party had already worked with it in the 1982 local elections, resulting in a memorable unemployment graph and the
slogan 'See what happens when you don't vote Labour!' Nick
Grant approached them in March 1983 for the local elections
and they evolved the 'Think Positive' slogan. With the
general election following immediately they were kept on.

The other recruit was Market & Opinion Research Inter-
national and its managing director, Bob Worcester. Labour
had used pollsters since the 1960s, Worcester since the 1970s.
They never polled on the lavish Tory scale, but Harold
Wilson had been a clear-eyed enthusiast and a clever user.
Wilson put the February 1974 victory down to Worcester's
recommendations to shift the party on to prices and to stick
to this as an issue. Yet the 1979 experience had been less
happy. The polls had merely underlined the inevitable and
Heffer subsequently described voting for using polls as the
decision he most regretted. Not a good augury, but wisely
MORI was now belatedly brought back into a relationship
always certain to provide more kicks than ha'pence. Michael
Foot had initiated contact in June 1982, postponed it to
December for want of money and signed contracts only in
February 1983. The first soundings, group discussions all
over the country designed to bring out the issues, images and
moods, were then carried out followed by a major panel sur-
vey.The gloomy results were relayed back to the campaign
committee, which had viewed their comprehensive indictment of party, policies and leadership with a mixture of
blank dismay and propensity to hide. Since the only intelli-
gent response to such an indictment was to change leader
and/or policy, Labour responded by restricting circulation of
the study and trying to forget it.

The announcement jolted their leisurely preparations into a more hectic pace. The campaign committee looked at the posters and pamphlets and authorised them. It was not happy with the slogan 'Think Positive', which had all the impact of a Pelmanism advert in the *Sunday Express*. Yet it was kept on because the agency seemed disinclined to think of any alternative at short notice and that put forward by Walworth Road Staff, 'Gi' us a job', was considered to cast an odd light on Labour's aspirations. 'Are you going to vote yourself out of a job?' worked better in the market research and that became a major theme. A more aggressive stance, quoting Margaret Thatcher's 'We will reduce unemployment to below one million' and adding 'Don't let them CON you again', was dropped after research showed women hating it and most people disliking knocking copy. With hindsight and having seen the impact of the Tory knocking, Wright considered he should have gone into the attack. Too late. Thus the agency under its general brief began to work on the advertising and the television and radio party politicals for which it had been made responsible.The Red Titanic headed out to stormy seas. Aneurin Bevan's vivid but probably inaccurate image was that fish rot from the head downwards.So did Labour's campaign. Michael Foot had never run an election campaign, showed no desire to do so and was weak on the two vital requirements. He was a spokesman, not a leader, speaking the language of the party and its declining bank of supporters, not the nation. He was inflexible, even obstinate, in his response to new challenges and situations. His response was to spray problems with words and hope they would go away. Though trusted, he did not trust, and though incapable of leading, he was determined that no one else should. He could not handle the press conferences as well as Denis Healey, yet always came. A sensible division of Labour, with Foot speaking to the party, Healey to the nation, was never arrived at.

Foot's instinct, encouraged by his advisers, was to throw himself into a whirl of activity well calculated to drive out minor considerations such as thought, calculation, even preparation. Accompanied by Jock Stallard on what looked like a Saga, in the sense of a pensioners' outing, he embarked on a massive tour campaigning in the only way he knew how, by orating to as many people as possible, compensating by activity for what he could not offer in leadership, experience or facility in the more useful arts of television and media manipulation. Since the speaker secretary, John Taylor, was ill throughout the campaign, the tours were arranged by the meetings unit: Joyce Gould, assisted by Andy Bevan. This produced subsequent accusations that Bevan had steered Foot to *Militant* candidates in Bradford, Coventry and the great metropolis of Brighton. Others argued that simple incompetence did that. The tour of the barren lands in the south was fixed before and places like Bradford certainly could not be avoided. The Tories made hay by publicising the platform stand with Pat Wall. Yet they would equally have publicised absence. The problem was therefore the longer standing of a party which had abandoned control over suitability of candidates. Thus Michael Foot addressed over a hundred meetings and did walkabouts most days, though at times they became carryabouts. He met far more people with far less protection or even preparation than any previous Labour leader.

A campaign needs a nucleus, a kernel of command, calculating and directing it. Michael Foot could not provide it. He was distracted by effort and exhaustion, frequently away, unable to be consulted and incapable, in urgent situations, of breaking the habits of a life time by giving clear, simple and binding answers or even delegating the job of giving them to someone who knew his mind. That job of interpretation had been easy with Jim Callaghan, whose mind ran on simple fairly straight tracks, but was impossible with a leader whose decisions were more like cushions bearing the impress of whoever had last sat on him. Michael preferred problems to go away. In election campaigns they come home to roost. The strain of going out seeking the public in penny packets distracted from the best and most effective way of reaching them by the million on television. Had Gladstone been alive he might have had more sense than to trudge round Midlothian, preferring the Saatchi–Thatcher technique of one visit as a media event followed by a fireside chat in a comfortable studio. Michael Foot was not so wise. Using TV properly needs thought and preparation, a relaxed confident approach, a strategy for questions and answers. Instead Michael Foot rushed round exhausted and confused, re-assembling in his head for each of the crucial TV interviews the gobbets of rhetoric, answer, information and disquisition which prop platform technique but look tired, dated and eva-sive on television.

There is no better insulation from reality than rushing out to meet it. Walkabouts introduce leaders to sweating camera crews, not people; they are an event, not an interchange. Party faithful at meetings are not a useful sounding board. They respond with warmth and affection, particularly to a leader who so clearly needed both, but insulate from reality even more. Mrs Thatcher was similarly out of touch but more graciously so, and she had a professional machine to tell her what to do and say. Her relaxed swan round the country, holding occasional meetings like middle-class Nuremberg rallies, concentrating on walkabouts and specially created 'tele-opportunities', was both an effective television cam-paign and a better preparation for other appearances. Government had been simplified to a technique of public relations. The lesson was not forgotten just when it was most useful. So Mrs Thatcher's hands hardly touched the people, her feet hardly touched the ground. To her Boswell daughter Carol, it seemed arduous. Yet Mother has always been a workaholic and with the load of normal business temporarily lightened, a swan around the country must have been a plea-sant change.

Labour needed the weather house technique of bringing the deputy leader forward, taking the leader back, as the weather changed to elections. Denis Healey fought an ener-getic and strenuous campaign. He and Michael Foot tried to present a team image. Yet there was too little trust on policy, particularly in the crucial area of nuclear disarmament. Michael declined to announce that he would hand over this area to Healey in government by putting him in charge of arms reduction. Yet neither could he bring himself to make the ringing declaration of unilateralist enthusiasm which would have sprung logically from his past. Labour paid the price in policy confusion for which the only parallel was the Tory split on free trade and tariff reform before the 1914–18 war. Then they too had ruined themselves in opposition, arguing over a policy which could only be decided in power.

Healey's role was frustrating, playing second fiddle in a campaign which he was better qualified to lead, watching a series of blunders which he, as the only serious campaigner at the top, would almost certainly have avoided. He fought an exhausting campaign in over eighty constituencies, starting in London with breakfast TV, a campaign committee each day, heading out by private plane to meetings, two or three a night, then back by plane late at night. He was under constant pressure to take a higher and higher profile. This pressure to excel – or rather exceed – put him in a more exposed situation, caused him to push both attack and gimmicks further and harder. Together with the strains of a sixteen-hour day, it may also have contributed to his major slip-up of the campaign, the attack on Margaret Thatcher as 'glorying in slaughter'. This throw-away remark at the end of a half-hour speech was inevitably seized on and exaggerated out of all proportion by a media eagerly waiting for Labour boobs. The reaction was immediate. Next day he withdrew but the damage was done. To be a second in command to an incompetent leader is a game in which the deputy can only lose and the question is only how badly. Upside gain was impossible. Michael Foot would not go. Only the greatest of ability fended off the downside.

A power vacuum at the centre left the Labour campaign without a brain. The National Executive could not supply it. The right-wing majority was feeling its way, uncertainly and moving far too slowly. Walworth Road (the name Labour had drifted into giving headquarters after the NEC had abandoned a name competition because the largest entry – three votes – was for 'Progress House') was not a happy place, ideologically divided with warring fiefdoms, competing ambitions and overworked officers. Jim Mortimer, a conciliator, not a strong man, failed to drive it forward. He was good and tough by reputation but learning a new job revealed neither quality. 'I know I don't take quick decisions but that's the way I am,' with little sensitivity to public moods, a lot for the trade unions. The agency could have contributed sense but was neither represented on the campaign committee nor brought together early enough with Bob Worcester. It also had a lot of catching up to do. The director of publicity was able but feeling his way, did not know the business, and his indecisions generated hostility from his own staff. So the campaign devolved on a series of units, each going its own way with little or no coordination. The national agent's office had its set routines and its own hierarchy. The research department was waging its own ideological war, happy to justify its prescriptions, but with no one to drive it or force it to examine its positions. The agency settled down to the arduous job of producing fifty minutes of television programmes, a considerable undertaking since most agencies do less than fifteen minutes a year. The shadow cabinet toured the country speaking on their specialisms with little attempt to coordinate themes or phrases, or even to strike the same chord at the same time, the one sure and effective way of getting messages and ideas through to the public by reiteration. The Conservatives used this cleverly, talking of 'one-sided disarmament'. Labour bungled the one advantage it could have had. The leader had his own staff, Dick Clements and others at Walworth Road most of the time and Tom McCaffery travelling. Yet their job was to sustain, and that meant defend, him. So Labour's was not one campaign but several working, often accidentally, under the same banner and not always that.

Labour began sixteen points behind the Tories – ominous and probably disastrous. No party had ever recovered that much in a campaign, yet there was still hope that the gap must close. It always had in the past and it did, indeed, begin to. There was even a plan, to hit hard on unemployment in the first week then, having got government on the defensive, to move on to the foreign and defence issues which could only be sustained by a strong economy and to conclude on the caring issues and the benefits in social improvement which growth and strength could confer. The strategy made sense. Money was no problem – at least £2.5 million was available. Bob Worcester, the best pollster in the business, pointed the task ahead by establishing the key areas and assessing in which Labour was ahead (few) and which behind. He urged building up strength on the doubtful issues and keeping off the danger areas, Falklands, defence, even the EEC, which his polls showed was a lost issue. To chart progress his regular polls – usually daily – were reported back to a polling committee of departmental heads plus Peter Kellner and Andrew Mackintosh. He then reported the deliberations to the campaign committee. This brought Labour information on a scale not enjoyed in 1979. With it came the opportunity to be both flexible and effective, provided it was used properly.

The promise was never fulfilled. The first week was successful though the press largely ignored Labour's unemployment theme, a failure which made it more difficult to be consistent in future. At the end of the week Labour ran into the one-third barrier, a level of support it could not cross, began to lose impetus and slip back, then came unstuck on defence. This danger was implicit from the start. On the release of the Campaign Document Denis Healey had pointed out the incompatabilities: negotiate with Polaris but also get rid of it; have no nuclear defence yet cut conventional defence spending; stay in NATO but throw out American nuclear weapons. At the press conference when Healey reserved his position on what would happen if negotiations failed, he had been rebuked by party chairman Sam McCluskie who, in his gentle sensitive way, had told Denis Labour would get rid of Polaris in five years. Michael Foot, though told about the deficiencies, had taken no steps to have them covered, so the technique used in the campaign document of placing contradictory sentences after each other was simply transferred to the manifesto without any attempt to see if the glue had set. On bases it read: 'This means the rejection of any fresh nuclear bases or weapons on British soil or in British waters and the removal of all existing nuclear bases and weapons thus enabling us to make a direct contribution to an eventually much wider nuclear-free zone in Europe. However, all this cannot be done at once.' On Polaris, 'We will propose that Britain's Polaris force be included in the nuclear disarmament negotiations in which Britain must take part. We will, after consultation, carry through in the lifetime of the next parliament our non-nuclear defence policy.' Putting the aging Polaris systems into negotiation was a sensible stroke and popular. It would have been equally effective to have argued only for non-escalation, for Trident and Cruise were not popular. Throwing nuclear weapons away 'in the life of the next parliament' undercut both and was widely unpopular.

The bomb was detonated immediately. Hostility to unilateral disarmament was so strong on Grimsby doorsteps that I immediately wrote to the three men concerned with defence to warn them what was happening, a warning they were also receiving from the polls and from other candidates. I received three different replies. John Silkin's simply said that he, Michael and Denis had agreed the policy and it was a good one, while Michael Foot re-emphasised his anti-nuclear commitment.

This situation brought out all the ambiguities in the relationship between Denis Healey, realpolitikian, and Michael Foot, lifelong disarmer. On Friday Healey drew up a new statement which Foot accepted on Saturday. It was then trailed for Monday's press conference, On Monday nothing was unveiled. Foot was holding it back to consult with fellow nuclear disarmer Jim Mortimer. Healey pressed and on Tuesday out came the statement: the Healey negotiating strategy was the party's. Michael Foot then amplified it and an audible sigh of relief went up; the window of vulnerability was boarded up. Next day came Jim Callaghan's blithe statement disassociating himself from unilateral nuclear disarmament and reviving the whole issue. As a former prime minister he was bound to emphasise his own consistency. Yet no one was clear whether he rushed to do so or was prodded into it by a persistent press. Since his remarks were circulated in advance, though not to Walworth Road, the former seems most likely. Press and the television now climbed back in through the re-opened window to pick through the rubble. Brian Walden devoted nearly two-thirds of his long Sunday interview with Michael Foot to the one issue. The headlines drove it home to an anxious public. No one could stay off it. Denis Healey continued his explanations that the next generation of weaponry did not need US bases in Britain so that the existing ones were going anyway. Michael Foot continued to harp on the issue and his own commitment but also stuck obstinately to the formula which he clearly regarded as a life raft, so desperately that some speculated that he had been nailed to it by the right. Shadow ministers such as Roy Hattersley argued that the party had lost on that subject and should drop it, meeting with an angry reaction from Michael Foot, unable to abandon the convictions of a lifetime. Foot spoke on other subjects usually on, or around, those arranged. Yet he also included ringing invocations of his concern for disarmament which inevitably got the headlines or the TV coverage, keeping the subject to the forefront. After obstinately stonewalling the pleas of the right up to the middle of the campaign on the Bank Holiday Monday he accepted the truth from someone he trusted: Judith Hart. 'Michael, you've lost on the nuclear issue. Drop it.' He did.

Getting out of such ruts with minimum damage rather than digging in is the responsibility of campaign strategy. Because its campaign was like a huge prehistoric reptile, lumbering body, small directing brain, and conditioned reflexes which evolution was rendering outdated, Labour could not respond. The daily campaign committees were chaotic. Up to thirty people, usually different each day, crowded into the general secretary's room at Walworth Road: shadow cabinet, National Executive, pollsters, officials. New every morning is thy committee so there was no continuity, much rehashing, always too many, always too hot, windows tight shut presumably to prevent the secrets leaking before the participants left. Each morning began with its commentary by Bob Worcester, with slides on the latest polls, his and everyone else's, clear, dry, understated, full of good advice, 'Don't say hospitals, say health service,' 'keep off defence.' Desultory questions followed. No one ever asked the big basic: 'Why is Labour sagging and the Alliance rising?' Discussion on the day's press conference followed, usually with a subject and speaker arranged the day before, often with a document to be circulated which, equally often, was not ready. Then the meeting drifted off into personal views, argument, recriminations. One observer considered that each person slid into a performance:

John Golding is the man of the people, the stranger who always has the last word in the argument in the pub; Peter Shore sounds more and more like an economics lecturer; Roy Hattersley like the garage mechanic who alone knows why the engine is making the funny noise and how much it will cost to put right. Neil Kinnock sounds more and more like the sports master who is sure that he is popular with the boys. The leader of the party agrees with each speaker in turn even when one directly contradicts his predecessor. When the last miracle man has finished the leader sums up at considerable length. His speech has all the symptoms of coherence: there are rises and falls and dramatic pauses, dismissive laughs, flashes of anger, stern emphases. But at the end it is difficult to discern what the leader has decreed. 'This is what we've been doing right all the way through this campaign, up and down the country and what we're going to do is go on saying it, the things we've been saying. And of course we're going to talk about other matters, pensions and other matters and that is the right way to go about it and I agree with the things that have been said, and it is right they should be said.' The sentence is interminable. Sometimes he nears the end, but scuttles back like a nervous child on the high diving board. No one is watching him, not even his courtiers. A series of low private conversation begins round the table. I try to read the leader's face, tired and grey but serene. He is the trustee of the hopes of millions of people for jobs, for peace, for a better life. If the polls are correct those hopes will not be realised: The people will be delivered into the hands of a government which will create millions more unemployed, ravage the welfare state, load Britain with new nuclear weapons. But the leader still looks serene. He has filled his destiny. It is enough just to be leader, even penned in this room full of smoke and quarrels and failure. Being leader is his revenge on Gaitskell and the fifties. By being leader he has kept the Labour Party safe from revisionism, safe from victory.

That was all that most days held time for. The conference itself was back in its old mausoleum Transport House, Smith Square, fifteen minutes away through rush hour traffic. Departure brought a compulsory end and usually arrival on time for the press while departmental heads met to act on any decisions it may have strayed into accidentally.

Towards the end of the campaign the atmosphere was one of sad, futile failure, party officials dazed and not comprehending what was happening, the right building a pent-up fury at the way things were being allowed to slide, others preparing excuses. Or positions. Above it all, hovering out of touch but bearing up well, the leader was slipping slowly into history while others prepared for the succession. This was not the stuff of which victories, even holding operations, are made. Yet it was all a logical conclusion of the years which had gone before. I tramped the streets of Grimsby assuring the doubtful that though Michael Foot may not be 'impressive on television' he was nonetheless sincere and like Attlee, a similarly unimpressive figure, he would prove a good committee chairman, adept at holding things together. In London he was belying it. The mess was private. Its consequences were all too public. Fortunately too the last few days did see things pulled more firmly together, a smaller nucleus, firm decisions, but too late.

It was not all unrelieved gloom, as a comic calendar numbering from 10 May shows:

Day Nine
Before the committee can proceed to its business the general secretary insisted on reading a letter from party chairman Sam McCluskie of the NUS. McCluskie was present but would rather have his views made coherent. Yesterday, though chairman, he had been stopped by Labour Party officials from going on to the platform at the press conference. He is not, of course, protesting for himself. Individual feelings don't matter. He is protesting for the trade union movement which had been insulted. The meeting listened, shuffled and moved on. McCluskie did not appear on the

platform, a downgrading which did not stop him catching the headlines next day by warning of political strikes if the Conservatives won.

Day Thirteen
The agency, filling its brief on security with a programme on law and order, defence having been dropped from the cocktail, included a 'brilliant' piece by John Mortimer filmed outside Wormwood Scrubs. At the last minute the Research Director in Walworth Road insists that it be cut *in toto* because it mentioned 'overflowing chamber pots'.

Day Seventeen
Jim Mortimer, hithertoo an excellent commander of the Press Conference announces 'At the campaign committee this morning we were all insistent that Michael Foot is the leader of the Labour Party and speaks for the Labour Party'

Day Twenty One
Williamsburg Conference Day. Labour's Press Conference was devoted to 'The Arts'. After strenuous protests about the relevance of Arts to Mammon it was agreed to organise another press conference that afternoon on Williamsburg. A grumbling Michael Foot cancels a children's function to be there. At the morning Campaign committee Bob Worcester's report on ten days to go reveals the gloomy news that where Labour had orginally been ahead only in one of five crucial areas such as 'best team' it had now slipped behind on that and caring and concern. On the issues, Labour had initially led on N.H.S., Education, Unemployment and Industrial Relations. It was now ahead only on two. Even there the gap had narrowed,. In the face of this gloom it was agreed to set up a new smaller committee with Roy Hattersley to give the campaign more direction. However another crucial weakness, the failure to monitor what the Tories were doing and saying in the same way as they were monitoring Labour, could not be remedied for lack of manpower. Without the same instant feedback the Labour Party was unable to respond immediately to everything the other side said and did.

Day Twenty Four

With the press now clamouring for visuals and very badly supplied, Ann Taylor, most photogenic of the front benchers, is brought down to provide them and give herself a boost in Bolton. Asked about the graphics the Press Director slips out looking worried. No graphics. A piece of white board, and felt tips to draw price changes on are hastily gathered. No drawing pins. Ann Taylor delivered her text reading and sitting down. She did not feature on television.

Day Twenty Six

The official press conference on pensions with – a good idea – four pensioners unfortunately all looking younger than the leader. Neil Kinnock organises his own press conference on education at a school indicating that 'every man for himself' is about to break out.

The rest of the campaign was no more than competent. By contrast with the shambles at the centre it managed to look good. The national agent's office, grossly overworked, kept the rusting Labour machine going. The research department, always more devoted to promoting socialist ideology than to praising the leadership and passing the ammunition, kept up a flow of documents. *Today*, the daily campaign guide, intended to supply candidates with facts, argument and suggested speech themes, was much less useful than it had been in 1979. The quarrying efforts of government departments were no longer available so the ratio of facts to argument was lower. Press advertising was adequate, though with some curious lapses, such as seed cast on the stony ground of the *Economist* or an advert comparing the cost of battleships with hospitals, which the campaign committee thought it had rejected but which still made its appearance. The television campaign was solid but dull, marred mainly by the nervous amateurism of much of the presentation, as unsure shadow spokesmen faced cameras like rabbits in headlights. Michael Foot played little part, though on one the agency was suddenly told to include him, with two days to go, and had to get a crew to go to Coventry and fit a hotel room out like Number 10 at inordinate cost. He appeared again at the end when hard work and long hours produced a Valium performance supposed to equate with statemanship. Others, among the better television performers, such as Denis Healey and Gerald Kaufman, either had to force themselves on to the party politicians or failed to get on at all.

The message got across. Yet it was not tied in with the rest of the campaign. Amateurism might have been attractive, compared with the slick professionalism of the Tory sales pitches, but the real enemy was the SDP: attractive leaders, presented in relaxed but ungimmicky settings in staid but effective party politicals. A great opportunity, worth perhaps £20 million to a party if bought at commercial rates, was not used as effectively as it should have been. Labour had not gone to the trouble, the preparation and the planning that the actual expenditure of such a sum would have forced it to do.

What benefits did Labour get from the professional advice which was more readily available than in 1979? Professionals provide a sense of reality, advice on tactics and skills in marketing which are essential to any campaign, for sausages or policies. They can turn out a competent result when all else is lacking. The agency did with broadcasts. In Labour's case this was not very good. The party is suspicious of professionalism. Jim Mortimer commented with amazement that the Tory Party had an advance man going ahead of the Queen-Empress to work out camera positions, shot angles, appropriate locations, events. 'Thank heayens we don't need to do that with Michael,' was his response. 'We're not that kind of party.' It showed: arrivals without crowds, cameras kept waiting, opportunities missed, prepared texts not delivered so that crews with deadlines took anything they considered appropriate. Alliance organisers had plenty of stories of Roy Jenkins arriving in shopping centres on half-day closing, but Conservative chaos, which clearly existed, for there were bitter arguments at Smith Square, was better concealed.

Ideologues in the party see polls as a capitalist plot, or as reducing politics to the level of giving people what they want. Such attitudes made Worcester's role more difficult, but only until confidence began to evaporate and people began to realise that disaster lay ahead. At that point they discovered a sudden interest in how to avoid it. Some commented that no one listened to Worcester. Others viewed his work as invaluable, suggesting themes, ideas for speeches, buzzwords and approaches which were invaluable, at least to those like Denis Healey and Roy Hattersley who used them. His services were also invaluable in helping the party to counteract the impact of the Audience Selection polls which, being telephone polls, overstated the Alliance by 3–4 per cent and thus helped the attempt to stampede the country into Alliance voting. Yet even here some thought this a disservice, leading people to assume that there was no bandwagon, when the real dispute was over how fast it was rolling. The verdict must be that the polls were essential. The party was right to use them. Yet it was not competent enough, nor well enough led, to get value for its own money.

Labour's 1983 election campaign was unique in recent political history. Leaders summed it up as 'a disgrace to a major party', 'a disaster' and 'not very good'. It resulted in a new phenomenon. Normally the party nationally has been able to offer a whole range of bonuses to local parties and candidates. A local party wages its constituency fight but looks for strength to the centre. The leader nationally has usually been more popular than the Labour Party. In 1983 both these factors were absent. The party dragged its components down. The leader lagged. In previous campaigns tours by leading figures have provided vital boosts. In 1983 tours concentrated on seats to be won but the real problem was those about to the lost and party processes were too cumbersome to switch once that was clear. In previous campaigns slogans such as 'Let's go with Labour' and 'You Know Labour Government works' have encapsulated a theme, even a mood. 'Think positive, Act positive, go to sleep' was eminently forgettable. In previous elections the national campaign gave a lead, even a coherence, to the patchwork of local campaigns. In 1983 they had to excuse, explain, climb out from under. For the first time since 1931 Labour candidates began to feel that they were surviving, if at all, through their own efforts and those of their local party, fighting in their own trenches, while the national campaign was rather like a distant Russian front in 1917, with daily news of fresh disasters. It undermined candidates, contradicting what they were saying, generating embarrassing questions.

The campaign in Grimsby was enthusiastic, lively, exciting, with a good response from the electorate, building a confidence no one observing the national scene could have felt. Candidates, like leaders, tend to be insulated from reality, absorbed in their own constituency, knocking on doors, dragging people away from the television and newspapers, actually interrupting the real campaign to wage their own. There were increasing frustrations: supplies of pamphlets which did not arrive, then were promised for 10 June and finally ended up in Great Yarmouth. A plea for visiting speakers produced Clive Jenkins and Tom Sawyer (without Huckleberry). No campaign handbook came but a supply of campaign suggestions which simply recycled the same sparse supply of facts endlessly.

Ignorance was bliss. To have known what was happening would have sapped morale. Yet it would also have forced me to realise what I did not understand until too late, that what I took for interest and concern about the issues, making it necessary to work harder for every vote, was really an electorate sidling away from Labour and looking for reasons to dismiss them, not for explanations of why they should reject the government. On the doorstep Michael Foot was an albatross. He amplified all Labour's problems, heightening difficulties by his obscurities, compounding failure by his lack of leadership, reinforcing the image of age and irrelevance by his very appearance. We could not win with Michael. Too late I took the action I should have taken months before and wrote to him suggesting that only he could rescue the party from imminent disaster by doing a Hayden, resigning on health grounds and letting another leader take over. We had no Bob Hawke but no one could have done worse than Michael. Since he was well protected from reality I marked the letter 'urgent' and 'personal' and asked for a written assurance that he had at least read it and considered it. No answer came.

The most extraordinary campaign in British electoral history maundered to a close. The issue was not the government but the opposition. The race was not over first place, but who was to be third. Most campaigns end with some kind of a judgement on the government of the day, backing its effort, warning it, throwing it out. A modern electorate, like a constitutional monarch, has the right to be consulted, the right to encourage and the right to warn, as well as the even more used right – for electorates are crueller and more powerful than constitutional monarchs – to throw out. In 1983 it opted to use none on the government, the last two on Labour. The final result was almost exactly the same gap between the two parties, up from 14 per cent to 15 per cent as at the start. Labour seemed to have run all that way, made all that effort, endured all that misery only to stand still. The Tories had lost slightly, Labour substantially. The third party, which everyone knew was not going to win, and which the great majority were clear was going to finish up with no more than a handful of seats, improved its poll rating considerably. Thus the election ended up not so much a judgement on the government as on the opposition, not an electoral choice but a vote against the two-party system itself. Compared with 1979 Labour had lost over a quarter of its previous vote. The Conservatives, despite a landslide majority of 144, were down 1.5 per cent in share of the vote and 2.6 per cent in share of the British enrolment, Yet because they had lost less than Labour, down 9.3 per cent on vote, 8.2 per cent on enrolment, the Tories donated only one vote to the Alliance to every three from Labour. The result was a continuance of the long dwindling in the Labour vote from its 1966 peak. It also took the third party vote to 25.4 per cent or 26.4 per cent in England, over the record figure of February 1974. The Conservative share was still fluctuating between three and four tenths of the total electorate.

By regions the pattern was of unusual uniformity. Everywhere the same trends were evident. The Tories gained in only two, the East Midlands and East Anglia. Labour lost everywhere, but most in those two areas. Both the Alliance vote and its gain were absolutely uniform. In only three regions, Scotland, Wales and the Northern Region, did Labour emerge even as the largest single party; it nowhere got the outright majority the Tory Party won in East Anglia, the South-east outside London and the South-west. Those

		Share of the total British electorate for each party		
		Labour	Conservative	Third Party	No Vote
	1959	34.6	38.5	4.7	21
	1964	34.6	33.1	8.8	22.9
	1966	37.2	31.5	6.6	24
	1970	31.6	33.2	5.5	28.1
(Feb)	1974	30.1	30.7	15.6	20.9
(Oct)	1974	29.3	26.8	13.7	27
	1979	28.8	34.2	10.8	23.8
	1983	20.6	31.6	18.9	27.3

regions typify the extent of Labour's decline and the extent to which 1983 drove it back to become a party not of the nation but of the declining regions – without any re-establishment of its position in the West Midlands, the worst hit region industrially. In the richest part of the country, where unemployment was lower, where such growth as occurred under Mrs Thatcher's system of government of the South-east for the South-east by the South-east, of 179 constituencies from the Wash to the Avon, Labour only won three, Bristol South, Thurrock and Ipswich, where Ken Weetch hung on by effective organisation supplemented by keeping the word 'Labour' out of his election leaflet, staying off policy and running as 'the man you know' rather than a Foot soldier. Over the Labour wastelands of the south the party won only 17 per cent of the votes against the Alliance's 29 per cent, coming third in 149 seats and losing deposit in half the constituencies.

Labour's dilemma now is that to win a bare majority it has got to win 117 seats and gain a swing of 12 per cent, the biggest ever in British political history. These might come from the 132 seats in which the party is still second, but to be able to govern it must win nine out of ten of them, and to be sure of a majority adequate for survival, it will need to strike into less habitable territory, the seats where Labour now comes an ignominious third. The dilemma is typified not by the national figures of which classes need to be won but by the actual seats Labour needs. Waveney in Suffolk is the seat Labour must have to get a majority of two. That means overcoming a Tory majority for James Prior of 14,298, and appealing to a town with 68 per cent owner-occupiers (as against 56 per cent nationally) only 0.5 per cent black or Asian, an unemployment level lower than the national average at 10 per cent (compared to 12 per cent nationally at census time) and a workforce in work which is doing very well thank you. Labour is not so much running an electoral race as praying for a miracle.

7 · Surveying the Wreckage

'We must not compromise with the electorate.'
KEN LIVINGSTONE

Election victory was always unlikely for Labour but there is always hope, particularly for a party which only half believed polls. The electorate had become more volatile but old allegiances, it was assumed, should reassert themselves. Moreover Labour began well, by the simple expedient of kicking off before the other teams were on the field. The Alliance were lingering in the doldrums, and the Conservatives were gently swanning along, posing as a government until the week after. So polls showed an immediate response. Conservative and Alliance shares held steady. Labour's share edged up, reaching a peak on 19 May. The universe was unfolding as it should. The gap closed though only very slightly. As it did the Conservative team came on to the field.

At this point, Labour's advance stalled and the party's share of the polls began to slip back. The next phase lasted for just one week, from 20 to 27 May, and reflected the impact of the Conservatives. The Tory share edged up, though only slightly, for it had remained remarkably steady through Labour's initial rise. The Labour vote slipped back to its initial level. The Alliance changed not at all. The final phase went on from the end of May up to the actual result on 9 June. The electorate responded slowly to the deadlock – an enthroned government, a stalled opposition – which had emerged. The Conservative vote rose slightly but not to its initial level. Labour slipped back from its early (but low) foothills, clearly having no chance of closing the gap. The Alliance began not to creep but to lurch up. The initial lurch from under a fifth to a quarter of the vote came right at the start of the week. From that point, the Alliance moved only very slightly indeed. The main question of the election was decided; the electorate was addressing itself to another: who should hold second place. People were adopting the kind of look previously seen in their eyes only at by-elections. The polls themselves tell the story and they are treated altogether, for differences of technique are minor and the pattern of the findings was very similar, running across the thirty-five orthodox polls and even across some of the findings of the telephone polls.

The campaign is reflected in table 3. The reaction against Denis Healey's 'glories in slaughter' attack on Mrs Thatcher is a blip in the Labour vote which came out more clearly in party polls done daily. Mrs Thatcher's statesman-like strutting (for a few brief hours) on the world stage produced a brief reward for the Tories, yet after that expensive, glossy campaign they still had not got themselves back to where they started. In this sense the Conservatives lost the election. But not as badly as Labour, for the dominant trend was Labour weakening, the Alliance strengthening in an amble, not a Gadarene stampede. The press, ever eager to kick Labour, kicked harder when it was down and went out of its way to build up the Alliance with screaming headlines about its surge and constant emphasis on those polls which reflected it. The same technique had been used in by-elections, most spectacularly in Bermondsey. There it gave the electors the information they needed to decide how to get the result they wanted: to stop Peter Tatchell. First define your hate object. Then provide the bricks to throw.

Britain is not, thank heavens, Bermondsey. People were being proferred the same information but it did not have the same relevance because it was on a national, not local, basis and even had the Alliance moved ahead of Labour, as it did in post-election polls, the result in seats – a massive Labour block coming from the older fiefdoms, a minute Alliance band – would have been much the same. Thus what was being fostered was merely the approach to elections as a form of horse-racing. What was proffered for Labour was the humiliation of coming third in that, while inevitably being second in seats. The press would have wished such a consum-

Table 3 *A calendar of polls*

Pre-election

POLL	FIELD DATE	CON %	LAB %	ALL %	CON LEAD %
Gallup	4 May	49.0	31.5	17.5	+17.5
NOP	6 May	47.0	34.0	18.0	+13.0
MORI	5 May	46.0	32.0	22.0	+14.0

General election period

POLL	FIELD DATE	CON %	LAB %	ALL %	CON LEAD %
MORI	10 May	46.0	31.0	21.0	+15.0
Harris	11 May	52.0	31.0	17.0	+21.0
Gallup	11–16 May	46.0	33.0	19.0	+13.0
MORI	12 May	49.0	34.0	15.0	+15.0
MORI	16 May	44.0	37.0	17.0	+ 7.0
NOP	16–17 May	49.0	31.0	19.0	+18.0
Harris	18 May	45.0	35.0	17.0	+10.0
MORI	19 May	46.0	37.0	16.0	+ 9.0
Marplan	20 May	47.0	34.0	18.0	+13.0
Gallup	20–23 May	48.0	33.0	18.0	+15.0
MORI	23 May	51.0	33.0	15.0	+18.0
NOP	23 May	52.0	33.0	14.0	+19.0
Marplan	23–25 May	47.5	32.5	19.0	+15.0
Harris	24–25 May	48.0	33.0	18.0	+15.0
Gallup	24–26 May	49.0	31.5	18.0	+17.5
Gallup	25–30 May	47.5	28.0	23.0	+19.5
MORI	26 May	51.0	29.0	19.0	+22.0
Harris	26–27 May	47.0	30.0	21.0	+17.0
Marplan	27 May	49.5	31.0	19.0	+18.5
MORI	31 May	44.0	32.0	21.0	+12.0
Marplan	30 May–1 June	47.0	30.0	22.0	+17.0
Harris	31 May–1 June	46.0	28.0	24.0	+18.0
Gallup	31 May–2 June	45.5	31.5	22.0	+14.0
MORI	2 June	43.0	32.0	23.0	+11.0
Harris	2–3 June	47.0	28.0	23.0	+19.0
Marplan	3 June	44.0	27.0	27.5	+17.0
NOP	3 June	47.0	29.0	23.0	+18.0
Marplan	6 June	47.0	26.0	25.0	+21.0
NOP	6–7 June	46.0	28.0	24.0	+18.0
Gallup	7–8 June	45.5	26.5	26.0	+19.0
Marplan	8 June	46.0	26.0	26.0	+20.0
NOP	8 June	47.0	25.0	26.0	+22.0
MORI	8 June	44.0	28.0	26.0	+16.0
Actual vote	9 June	43.5	28.3	26.0	+15.2

mation. Yet it was a confidence trick, albeit one which was only possible because Labour and the two-party system were so unpopular.

The nature of the electoral decision had more to do with the actions of the Labour Party and its flagging campaign than any process of manipulation. Asked whether their final decision was influenced at all by the polls, only 5 per cent told Gallup it was, though it is also clear that the majority of the country, 61 per cent knew what the message of the polls was: a massive Tory lead. Clearly Labour was not going to make it; indeed as many as a third thought that Labour was actually in third place. All this must have encouraged the feeling that a Labour vote was a wasted vote, a feeling also encouraged by the Audience Selection telephone surveys. All had an implicit bias against Labour, fewer of whose supporters have telephones, and in favour of a middle-class party such as the Alliance. On the published figures, the first bias was worth 3 per cent, the second 4 per cent, making them useful to anyone interested in boosting the Alliance. By coincidence the Alliance employed Audience Selection for its own polling. Their published polls were carried out for TV AM and the *Sun*, both more inclined to use a cut-price poll but neither particularly unfavourable to a Conservative Party certain to benefit if its opposition were fighting each other rather than the government. With the single exception of one aberrant NOP poll on election eve, no reputable poll put the Alliance significantly ahead of Labour. All, however, acknowledged that the gap was close, as, by the end of the campaign, it clearly was.

In February 1974 the last third-party upsurge had seen the Liberals, though starting from a lower base than the Alliance, make less ground in the campaign. They were also treated less seriously by the media. Perhaps, with Jeremy Thorpe and his hovercraft, deservedly so, but the role had been similar. A third-party draws most from whichever of the two major parties is in the greatest difficulties. In previous contests when the Liberals had advanced this was usually an incumbent Conservative government losing support. In 1974 the opposition Labour vote had been stronger because of the tense industrial situation.

Now the Conservative vote was stronger, Labour's more vulnerable. What happened reflected this. The Alliance was more attractive than Labour. It picked up more of the late deciders: 45 per cent of deciders in the campaign against 31 per cent to the Tories, 20 per cent to Labour and 53 per cent of those deciding 'in the last few days' against 23 per cent Tory and 22 per cent Labour. Its image improved. At the start of the campaign, 20 per cent told Gallup that they thought 'most people' had a favourable image of it, 54 per cent un-favourable. Comparable figures for Labour were 25 per cent and 62 per cent. At the end of the campaign the favourable proportion was 36 per cent, unfavourable 37 per cent, and the Labour figures declined to 17 per cent and 70 per cent. Thus while it was no powerful magnet, and only a fifth of Alliance voters identified strongly with it, compared with two-fifths from the other parties, the Alliance looked attractive, and three-quarters of those who went from Labour to it preferred both its leaders and its policies to those of their former party. Meanwhile Labour was unattractive so that 75 per cent of Labour defectors to the Alliance gave negative reasons for their vote, compared with 63 per cent of Conservative defec-tors. Asked which was stronger, liking of the Alliance or dis-like of Labour and Tory, 65 per cent of Labour defectors said the latter, as did 72 per cent of first-time voters who opted for the Alliance. On these figures the Alliance vote looks to have been a drift, facilitated by the relative attractiveness of the two sides, not a positive attempt to turn to them to stop the Conservatives. That drift hurt Labour more than the Con-servatives at a time when Labour was the only alternative which could turn out the government. It was therefore a sim-ple lack of enthusiasm for Labour.

The problem is not why was the Alliance so attractive, but why Labour was putting people off. That decline centred on performance. As early as 26 May, 46 per cent gave MORI the opinion that the Labour party had 'got worse' in the cam-paign, 8 per cent thought that it had improved. The Alliance figures were 14 per cent and 23 per cent. This failure under-lined doubts about Labour which had been there before but were not as clearly focussed until the election campaign. Michael Foot did not help. At the start of the campaign, a

MORI survey indicated that while the Tories held a substantial lead it dropped to level pegging when people were asked how they would vote if Denis Healey were leader. A similar question at the end and after Healey's 'slaughter' remark produced no significant alteration of voting intention but by then the damage was done. Michael Foot's standing began low. On the *Sunday Times* panel only 14 per cent thought he would make the best prime minister and 65 per cent were dissatisfied with him. It never rose. The proportions at the end were 15 per cent and 65 per cent. While 27 per cent had not seen him on television, the same proportion missing the blessings of Mrs Thatcher, twice as many – 37 per cent – said that he did not increase support for his party as those who thought as he did. Yorkshire Television's marginal seat MORI survey found only 6 per cent saying that Michael Foot's leadership made them 'more inclined' to vote for Labour. Seven times as many said it made them 'less inclined'. Gallup found only 13 per cent picked him as the best potential prime minister, 63 per cent as the worst and under half of Labour voters picked him as the best, as many choosing David Steel or even Roy Jenkins. Indeed among Labour defectors as few as 4 per cent put him best. Labour voters were more non-hostile to Maggie than loyal to Michael.

The ideologues and pundits like a clear contrast between parties having clear and sharply contrasting policies. Their prejudices were gratified in 1983 but the public liked the situation less. It has long been more doubtful about Labour's policies than the Conservatives' and now that there were more of them it liked them less, though the dwindling number of Labour supporters liked them more, a self-reinforcement phenomenon typical of declining parties. The pattern of reaction to policies as measured by MORI is shown in the table on p. 139.

Conservative policies, though few, were popular. Alliance policies, at least on PR and incomes policy, were popular though not widely associated with the party. Labour, which was taking the initiative on a wider range of issues, found its policies all unpopular. Even EEC withdrawal, thought to be Labour's populist issue, counted against it. Hostility to the

Policy	All electors %		Labour supporters %	
	Support	Oppose	Support	Oppose
Tory				
Abolish GLC and met counties	36	31	25	41
Base Cruise in Britain	52	34	30	57
Greater control over council spending	62	24	49	36
Secret union ballots for election	61	22	47	31
Labour				
Take Britain out of EEC	30	56	53	30
Import controls	61	22	66	16
Borrow to expand the economy	26	58	48	33
Cancel Trident	35	38	54	27
Remove delay from Lords	24	48	39	26
Get rid of Polaris	26	59	N/A	N/A
Get rid if Russians reduce theirs	50	33	N/A	N/A
Establish Prices Commission	80	20	N/A	N/A
Sell off BL and BSBC	57	43	N/A	N/A
Alliance				
Incomes policy	45	23	47	22
Introduce proportional representation	40	18	36	20

EEC had been diffused rather than strong and the mobilis-
ation of fear (largely uncountered by the Labour Party)
easily turned it round on an issue which was not thought to
be particularly important, a background grumble, not a
burning cause. Thus the only popular issues were those on
which the party was ambiguous, such as Polaris, when the
pollsters felt obliged to include two policies, both
Labour's. Giving it up in return for Russian concessions
was acceptable. So were policies Labour never got round
to arguing such as import controls or the Prices Commission. The uphill fight on its major and unpopular policies,
all of which had to be explained and argued, dissipated
energies.

In specific areas of policy, Labour was in a better position.
MORI asked marginal seat electors which party had the best
policies in various areas (see table on p. 140). Labour lagged
on four, including defence, to which Michael Foot devoted
disproportionate effort. These helped to inflate the issue out

	Rank	Con %	Lab %	Alliance %	Other/None/ DK %
Defence and disarmament	2	45	20	14	21
Education	4	34	27	13	26
Inflation and cost of living	3	47	22	12	19
Law and order	3	41	17	11	31
National Health Service	3	26	42	13	19
Pensions	5	29	37	12	22
Unemployment	1	28	32	16	24

of proportion. In 1979 only 2 per cent mentioned it to Gallup, in 1983, 38 per cent. On the nuclear aspect the Conservatives began with a large lead, with 19 per cent more in the *Sunday Times* panel thinking that Conservatives had the best policies. At the end of all Labour's efforts that lead was 27 per cent.

Yet Labour also led on three issues. These included unemployment, supposedly the major issue of the election. Here the lead was narrow. By the end of the campaign it had almost vanished. Even where the public was inclined to think highly of the approach, they had little faith in Labour. Asked by Gallup whether there would be more unemployment or less if Labour got in, 24 per cent said more, 38 per cent less. The main problem was the competence of the leader, whose image spilled over to his team, for only 25 per cent had 'great' or 'considerable' faith in the ability of 'Labour politicians to deal wisely with Britain's problems'; 44 per cent had 'little' or 'very little', and 27 per cent 'none', an image of incompetence exceeded only by the SDP's statesmanlike team. People put unemployment high on the problems list. Yet it is questionable how deeply they felt about it: 50 per cent thought it a bad thing, but 44 per cent thought it could be justified in a period of adjustment and 68 per cent, given the choice of how to tackle it, thought it better left to companies. 29 per cent thought it best done through government. Attitudes to the unemployed were ambiguous. Lingering remnants of the old 'scrounger' critique could still be discerned: only 6 per cent told Gallup that 'most' or 'some' were in the unemployed ranks 'through their own fault' but 43 per cent felt that an ambiguous 'some' were and 47 per cent thought that 'most' or 'some' could get a job if they tried. The public accepted much of what Margaret Thatcher was saying on an issue which was still a vague concern, not a direct and salient one. Gallup found only 13 per cent who had been hit by unemployment themselves, only 21 per cent experiencing it in the family. Two-thirds were totally unscathed and reflecting the economic gap emerging between those in work and those out of it. 51 per cent expected the economy to get better in the coming year and only 23 per cent expected it to get worse.

The public was largely unconvinced that Labour policies would work, because they shared Mrs Thatcher's piggy-banking approach to economics, disapproving of borrowing to finance expansion and feeling fatalistic about unemployment: 84 per cent of the *Sunday Times* panel felt that whatever government did numbers of unemployed would remain over 2 million, while 60 per cent felt it impossible to reduce unemployment substantially without a lot of inflation. However, the same proportion thought that government policies were 'not fair to all concerned'; yet asked whether the government was handling the economic situation correctly, 45 per cent thought they were and 46 per cent did not. In the long term, 58 per cent of the *Sunday Times* panel felt Tory policies 'will improve the state of Britain's economy'. The manner of economic policy, the courage, the confidence, attracted them while only 20 per cent of the *Sunday Times* panel thought Labour could reduce unemployment to under a million, 75 per cent thought it could not. It was a question of perceived competence.

The disaster which struck Labour came as a result of four years of decline. All the factors which conditioned attitudes were there before the campaign had begun. Asked by MORI early on if anything would change their minds and make them vote Labour, half non-Labour supporters said 'nothing'. Among the remainder 10 per cent said if 'Labour were more united', 9 per cent a new leader, 9 per cent less extremism and 9 per cent 'if I thought Labour could reduce unemployment' and 7 per cent less power for the unions. All these learned reactions were reinforced and in the *Sunday Times* panel, 30 per cent thought Labour 'extremist' in April, 42 per cent at the end compared to 19 per cent and 26 per cent for the Tory Party. Only 18 per cent felt Labour had 'sensible' policies, 32 per cent felt this of the Conservatives and 30 per cent of the Alliance. The result was a Labour decline among all sections of the population.

How groups voted (MORI)

	Con %	Lab %	All %	% of the population	Lab loss since Oct 1974	Con lead	Con swing 1979–83 %
	Shares of the vote						
All voters	44	28	26	100	−12	+16	4.5
Men	42	30	25	48	−13	+12	4.5
Women	46	26	26	52	−12	+20	4.0
18–24	42	33	23	13	− 9	+ 9	4.0
25–34	40	29	29	20	− 9	+11	3.0
35–54	44	27	27	32	−15	+17	3.0
55+	47	27	24	34	−13	+20	5.5
ABC 1	55	16	28	40	− 3	+39	2.0
C2	40	32	26	31	−17	+ 8	4.0
DE	33	41	24	29	−16	− 8	3.5
Trade unionist	31	39	29	25	−16	+ 8	5.0
Non-unionist	48	24	25	75	−11	+24	3.0
Unemployed	27	47	24			−20	1.0
Working	45	27	26			+18	2.0
Owner occupiers	52	19	28			+33	1.0
Council house	26	47	24			−21	4.5
OAP	51	25	23			+26	2.5

'If a man isn't a socialist when he is twenty then he hasn't a heart and a Tory when he's forty he hasn't a head.' it used to be said. Young and old belie it: in the BBC Gallup survey Labour actually came third among new voters. When half the children leaving school would not get jobs, half the young unemployed did not vote and a special MORI analysis showed that of those unemployed who had, 27 per cent voted Conservative, 24 per cent Alliance and 47 per cent Labour.

Class is ceasing to be the most clear test of allegiance, not because it is no longer relevant, but because Labour's basic support has eroded so far – unemployment has failed to polarise society in the way that the left had assumed it would. The unskilled and semi-skilled remained loyal, but the skilled workers dropped away, a fall which mainly took place in 1979 and has not been reversed. The middle-class electors who stayed loyal to Jim Callaghan in 1979, when 24 per cent voted for him, now give Labour only 16 per cent largely because the SDP took middle-class votes from Labour. Trade unionists, inevitably becoming more middle-class, are very evenly divided. Reluctant to vote Tory, they are more inclined to support the Alliance than any other section of the population, a proportion which was even higher among middle-class trade unionists, particularly women.

Only among unskilled working-class trade unionists did Labour achieve a 50 per cent share of the vote. The main differentiating factor in terms of allegiance was the simple test of home-ownership, with that 59 per cent of the public owning their own home giving Tories a 33 per cent lead, while the shrinking base of council-house tenants provided Labour with a 21 per cent lead. This pattern was the more striking among working-class home-owners in groups C2, D and E, where the Tories had 21 per cent lead over Labour compared with council-house tenants in the same class where Labour's lead was 25 per cent.

The Alliance emerged, as the Liberals before them, as the most classless of the parties, evenly spread among the social groups, with an average gain of 14 per cent over 1979 and 7 per cent over 1974, highest among the over 55s at 10 per cent and lowest among the 18-to-24 age group at an actual loss of 4 per cent with a record gain of 13 per cent over October 1974 among trade unionists. Most of this gain was at Labour's expense. The BBC Gallup poll brings out the pattern of transfer in its question on 1979 vote compared with that of 1983:

| 1983 | Change since 1979 (Gallup) | | | | |
	Con %	Lab %	Lib %	No vote %	Too young %
Con	77	7	14	22	28
Lab	4	63	9	12	17
Ali	13	22	72	14	20
Other	—	1	—	—	2
NV	6	7	5	52	32

Thus over a third of Labour's previous voters switched, compared with under a quarter of the Conservatives and just over a quarter of the Liberals. Most of Labour's loss was donated to the Alliance. Yet Labour was also losing direct to the Tories at twice the rate they lost to Labour and to abstention, though no more to this than other parties. Those who moved to the Alliance were slightly more likely to be women than men, more young than old, for the party did worst among the over 65s. In social terms the movement to the Alliance was remarkably even over the whole social range. As many people gave positive reasons for voting for it as among Labour voters but tactical voting certainly strengthened the Alliance: 26 per cent in the *Sunday Times* panel said at the start they would consider another party if their chosen one had no chance in that constituency, 28 per cent at the end. The chosen alternative for two-thirds was the Alliance. Yet it may also have lost for the same reasons. When MORI asked if Alliance supporters would vote for another party if theirs looked like coming third, as many said Tory as Labour. Motives can only be guessed at but when Gallup asked Alliance voters whether they were influenced by various factors, 'extremists in Labour Party' was the largest single reason given by 33 per cent, and 34 per cent of those moving from Labour, followed by 'disunity in the Labour Party' (25 per cent and 22 per cent) and 'prevent the Conservatives winning' (21 per cent and 28 per cent), indicating that at least part of the incentive was a loss of faith in the Labour Party or a candidate who was not going to make it.

The Conservatives held three-quarters of their 1979 vote, Labour lost 37 per cent, well over half of it to the Alliance.

The only consolation was that in the minds of some the aberration was only temporary. Asked by Gallup, leaving aside that particular election, how they thought of themselves generally, 40 per cent said Conservative, 34 per cent Labour and the Alliance was down to 15 per cent. Yet even this put Labour down 4 per cent on May 1979 when it had actually been ahead despite the temporary 'swing', the Conservative share up 3 per cent and the Alliance up 2 per cent. The deserters may have been like Little Bo Peep's sheep but to leave them alone was no guarantee that they would come home, dragging their tails behind them.

8 · Back to the Drawing-board

The right wing's main points of support are some union leaders and the parliamentary party. That is why the bourgeoisie set such great store on the independence of the parliamentary party from control of the rank and file. They also have an important base amongst councillors and particularly in moribund GCs and wards. As these renew and revitalise themselves on the basis of events the support for the right wing will tend to dwindle and disappear. The right will become more and more an unimportant rump inside the Labour Party without credit and without a future.

MILITANT

It was not one thing that had gone wrong, one subject of blame. It was everything. The SDP had harmed Labour yet that bitterness went back to 1981. Split votes had cost seats but that was a product of re-selection. The leader had been a liability but he had been chosen on 1980's motives. The policies had weakened the appeal but they had been put together from 1978. The party had presented a general image of division, incompetence, left domination, but that was a sedimentation, with the 1981 deposit particularly heavy. The electorate had not delivered a verdict on Labour's election campaign. It had rejected the party's last four years.

By their post-mortems shall ye know them. Summing up what has gone wrong and assessing its causes is a test of understanding and the necessary pre-condition for progress. It was a test Labour failed. The first reaction was inevitably one of stunned dismay. The second was a dredging round for explanations and excuses, often invoked as ammunition as much as explanation. An amazing array of both were conscripted but they were brought into service of sides, not the whole party. And all were partial. Nowhere was there a dawning realisation that for four years Labour had been marching obstinately and painfully down the wrong road. A summation had to be made. It was too painful for a bemused party to do.

First attempts to explain the disaster centred on a leader who had not certainly been an asset but who was chosen for what he was by the party itself and whose main contribution had been to compound all Labour's own problems and adverse images. While mouthing loyalty and praising with faint damns, Michael Foot was quietly pushed into history without any thought of the consequence of plunging the party into a leadership contest before it could even get its head straight on more basic problems. Union leaders whose silence had helped Michael Foot to keep a job he could never live up to now dropped him without dignity. David Basnett announced that the leader should be changed quickly, suggesting that it should skip a generation, thus callously demolishing both Foot and Healey. Michael Foot, who had promised Denis Healey that he would be fully consulted before any retirement decision, allowed his own announcement to be pre-empted by Clive Jenkins. Terry Duffy, immune to the joke current in union circles that Mickey Mouse was wanting a Terry Duffy watch for Christmas, endorsed Kinnock. So did Jenkins on behalf of ASTMS. Nothing in his short leadership became Michael Foot less than the leaving of it. When the party needed to learn the lessons of what had gone wrong and to look for ways out of it, Michael Foot offered no guidance and instead plunged the party into a totally distracting leadership election. When his greatest achievement had been to bring soft left, centre and right together, and to isolate the hard men, he allowed the party to be polarised. When an impending election and the right's last stand on the NEC could have been used to carry through early and necessary constitutional changes, and to complete the drive against Militant, all this was forgotten. The party was plunged into using again an elective machine which had been discredited in 1981 and could hardly be much improved two years later. The rush to judgement before union membership could even think about the matter, let alone express their views, became almost indecent, giving a clear indication that the trade union leadership had learned nothing and forgotten nothing about an electoral college supposed to make leadership elections more democratic. Once again the TGWU opted to take the decision cheaply and chose Neil Kinnock. Others consulted – more of them than the first time – yet most in limited fashion. Some were as comic as the UCW which simply decided to vote Kinnock/ Hattersley and invited members who did not like this to write in and protest. If those who live by the post don't have postal ballots who would?

When the party needed it most, there was to be no leadership at all. A discredited leader sitting in his bunker meant there could be no new election for PLP executive lest the two front-running candidates, Hattersley and Kinnock, finished up 5th and 7th. The Booth vacancy could not be filled, the dead wood could not be trimmed, and that meant the fifteen front-bench vacancies could not be filled either. Similarly the PLP, which desperately needed reorganising to be an effective opposition, could not sharpen its own attack by immediately developing subject groups as speaking teams. The party was to drift on without any organised attempt to give point to its discussions or lead to its deliberations, just at the moment when the government was at its point of maximum vulnerability. They would never have done the same for Labour.

Nor was there much clear thinking on what had gone wrong. Those most implicated had least to say. Michael Foot read a prepared speech to the Parliamentary Labour Party suggesting that the policies were right and that 'when you fight the next election you will find quite a lot of good guidance in the manifesto on which we fought . . . those are the themes that are going to be vindicated'.

The hard left were more implacable: 'the policies' were a life raft. The views of the rank and file could not be wrong. So they must have been betrayed. *Tribune* promptly named its Guilty Men, the Shores and the Hattersleys who had created the impression that Labour was divided and permeated by alien Marxists. Neither the weekly nor its contri-

butors showed symptons of dawning reality. It was early for
the slaughter of sacred cows. Yet to build an ideological pen
to protect them was another matter. Ken Livingstone hinted
darkly that the policies had been compromised and promptly
exited from the debacle by the very door John Golding had
tried so hard, and so disastrously, to close: the leadership
had not campaigned on the policies. Tony Benn was more
original; the election was a triumph:

> . . . for the first time since 1945 a political party with an
> openly socialist policy had received the support of over
> $8\frac{1}{2}$ million people . . . it is indeed astonishing that socia-
> lism has reappeared once more upon the national
> agenda and has such a large vote when you consider the
> obstacles that had to be overcome . . . the 1983 Labour
> manifesto commanded the loyalty of millions of voters
> and a democratic socialist bridgehead has been estab-
> lished from which further advances in public under-
> standing and support can be made.*

In the early stages of European contact in the Pacific false
prophets persuaded cargo-cultists to build dummy airstrips
or to drill with wooden rifles to bring 'cargo', the goods and
technologies they wanted from the west. The cargo never
came but the prophets always had good explanations:
instructions had not been followed minutely enough,
someone had not had enough faith, the Livingstone view, or
the cargo had come and no one had noticed, the Benn view.
The prophets always kept the support of a diminishing
number of people, indeed the John Frumm movement
lingers in Tanna today, yet the eight million people voting for
socialism did not explain the massive vote for Thatcherism or
just under eight million voting for what Tony Benn presumably regards as a middle-class cargo cult. Unless the people
were mad, or duped – both dangerous views for the nation's
top democrat.

The more realistic, left and right, had a range of explanations but a common theme. Whatever each section or indi-

* The *Guardian*, 23 June 1983.

vidual had discerned as the faults of the party in the years
before were the causes of its downfall. Being the Labour
Party, explanations centred on policy, either the substance or
the sales. Traditionally after a defeat there are immediate
demands for making the policy relevant to the 1970s or the
1980s, or whatever decade, without saying how. That precedent was duly followed:

> There is still a fund of sympathy for our socialist values
> waiting to be tapped. Large majorities back the idea
> that income and wealth should be more fairly distri-
> buted, that workers should be given more say in the
> running of their enterprises and that education, health
> and welfare services should be adequately maintained.
> This suggests not that we should adjust our attitudes to
> what people think but that we should highlight those
> issues on which we have the widest support. (Giles
> Radice, *Guardian*, 15 July 1983.)

> One of the most disappointing features of the recent
> campaign was our failure to offer a different vision of
> society a different set of moral values. It was this failure
> more than anything else which revealed the fatal loss of
> confidence at the heart of Labour's position . . . the
> labour movement has been caught short, forced to rum-
> mage round in a sort of historical junkshop where the
> only ready-made ideas are a clapped-out reactionary
> dogma which was barely relevant to the 1930s, let alone
> the 1980s. (Bryan Gould, *Guardian*, 24 June.)

> People have to be won over to a view of the world in the
> 1990s which makes them believe that our resources can
> be used in a sensible and humane way and restores their
> faith in equality and justice as attainable and desirable
> goals. (David Blunkett, *Guardian*, 15 July.)

> Put bluntly, our striking success in building support for
> left policies within the labour movement has been paral-
> leled by a crashing failure to mobilise support for those
> policies in the electorate . . . unfortunately the hector-

ing style of appeals to solidarity and group discipline
handicaps us in addressing an electorate who
increasingly want to be persuaded and convinced.
(Robin Cook, *Guardian*, 1 July.)

Like Tony Benn, all viewed it as a problem of socialism, the
right considering that a distorted version had been put before
the public, the left arguing that it had been badly sold.
Neither considered the more basic problem. Either there was
no useful agreed definition of socialism or the public did not
want anything to do with it. A party discussing what had
gone wrong in terms of socialism was inevitably turning
inward, the very process which had brought disaster in the
first place. Rather than say boldly what it actually thought,
that the policies had been disastrous, the right hinted that the
emphasis should be shifted. The left, as puzzled as the
designer of the Ford Edsel at the public's reluctance to buy,
insisted that new methods of promotion, or more time,
would do the trick. Both were right and wrong. Policy is only
the outward and visible sign of the internal state of the party.
All that the 1983 policy said was that the short-sighted left
had won the power struggle in the party and had no higher
objective than cramming in everything it wanted while the
going was good. The right, unhappy with what was being
foisted on it, had sold the product coolly and too *sotto voce*
to make it credible. Yet to protest at this was really to
demand another Labour Party. A party which is not united
can't develop or sell policies.

The real problem is wider than policy. To concentrate on
one aspect is to argue that Labour could be saved by a coat
of varnish here, a re-emphasis there, a new sales force of
knights in white collars. The old basics have failed; Crosland-
dite social democracy looked dated because of its inability to
provide the growth on which all else is predicated. The alternative, Marxist radicalism, is even more dated, forcing the
party into an inflexible mould profoundly unattractive to the
public. In the mid-1980s Labour has to accept that Marx is
dead, Crosland is dead and Tony Benn isn't feeling too good.
Yet policies are not born from systems of political thought,
however profound. If they do spring fully armed from the

head of any guru they are almost certain to be disastrous as well as dangerous. A manifesto reflects a party which must be healthy before it can provide an effective one. This is a question of changing the party before the policies can be improved. Much needs to be done about the structure of the house before the wallpaper goes up.

Structure is the problem. Labour's structure cut it off from the forces for progress and the wide and deep discontents generated by the Thatcher counter-revolution. It focused the party on its own internal preoccupations instead of being permeable or drawing those discontents in through roots and osmosis. The structure has turned the struggle between left and right, inevitable in a party of progress, from a battle of ideas to a struggle for power in which who ran the machine became more important than how: serious discussion of serious issues the public will accept. But not power struggles. Structure has rooted Labour to the declining forces in society, stifling change and adjustment, and turning it from a lively exciting breeding ground for new ideas, welcoming them from wherever they came, to a protectionist force justifying the argument of vested interests. An ideological structure shackles Labour to the unpopular and declining trade unions, not in a useful stimulating way which gives the benefits of their shrewd pragmatic common sense and the ability to talk to and lead their members, but in the most cumbersome inefficient way making for delayed decision, a preoccupation with their interests, not the party's, a lack of trust compounded by a desperate requirement for them to intervene, yet making that intervention clumsy, counterproductive and inept. In short, structure makes Labour inflexible, cumbersome and introspective when it should be a set of roots in society. It holds the party back when it should be a machine with which to win. It becomes an obstacle or burden when it should be a boost.

The original purpose of party organisation was to carry the party to power, not as a handmaiden of the head maiden, as in the Tory Party, but as part of a team effort, then to keep the party in power true to its principles and its partners, putting the long-term view to offset governmental preoccupation with the short term, keeping the party in touch with the public by acting as its roots in the community. Now both these roles are much less important. A party achieves power not because people knock on doors but because of its success or failure in a media campaign which is open to it as of right and reaches people in their homes without the intermediary of the party. The party in parliament knows the public mood not through the filter of a party, which colours everything with its own prejudices, and is useless at quantifying, but through the accurate barometer of the polls. The tug to principle is less useful because the roots are withering as membership falls, and the principles are less and less relevant to reality. The functions of party are less necessary. Yet the outside party has grown more powerful, distracting leaders from the wide public to petty internal preoccupations, becoming a public stage for a licenced and clamorous opposition, proferring a built-in battleground on which leaders must fight or be humiliated, and possibly both. Party leaders have something more important to do with their time than wrestle in mud with Sam McCluskie, trade insults with Dennis Skinner, who is by no means as lovable in the NEC as he is in the House, and explain the facts of political life in simple terms to whoever is the current representative of the Young Socialist façade for *Militant*. Indeed the party should not need back protection against its own people. The organisation, once an aid, has become a positive distraction, sidetracking the party from the electorate to an internal civil war which can become totally absorbing.

The structure is deadlocked. It is concerned with power rather than reality. Issues are never considered on their merits in the Labour Party; which policy is right or relevant, what leader is best for the purposes of the party, whether a decision is fair and defensible. They are viewed exclusively in terms of power, who benefits and how. Does this strengthen the left or the right? Will this vote persuade that side to go along on that issue? In this complex and cumbersome balance of forces justice is neither done nor seen to be done. Everything is up for grabs, for compromises, deals and fixes which have little to do with the issues involved, everything to do with the balance of power and forces. All this enforces the internal preoccupation which has been Labour's main weakness for a decade and has caused the party to become more and more sect-like. Organisation makes the party inward-looking not outward-going, more concerned with the balance of forces in its structure than with reaching people, speaking to an internal audience not the vast world outside, winning votes in the party not outside it. Any party preoccupied with its organisation is out of touch with the nation. A party pre-occupied with it to this extent is out of touch with reality. The only basis of success for Labour is that its policies, people and principles should broadly represent and be acceptable to the people for whom it claims to speak. The introverted, all-absorbing complexities of the structure we have built up totally preclude this, giving Labour all the endearing charac-teristics of a sect, except that its eyes are on Walworth Road rather than heaven and it lacks fire and zeal. The structure drags eyes down, converting the simple words of the sermon on the mount to the complex circumlocutions of composite 56 or the evasions and assertions of *New Hope for Britain*.

What needs to be done is clear but as usual the problem is to whom is it clear and what power they have to do anything about it. The party does not accept political science lectures with quite the same joy with which it hears appeals to socia-lism. Vested interests have shown themselves impervious to the interests of sense or the party when it conflicts with their own, and the unions, with the power to secure change – slowly – have neither clear ideas nor agreement on what. Better therefore to opt for the softly approach, getting back to a workable structure in stages, rather than demand what sense dictates, a structure like the Conservatives where the leader controls the electoral machine and the outside party is independent.

Such an approach means another long diet of consti-tutional reform, distracting attention from the real fight against government. Unfortunately since the reforms already carried have done so much damage, and since there is no possibility of revival while the party is locked into the same disastrous introspection, there is no alternative but to modify them. At least the path of sense should now be more clearly picked out. The scale of the 1983 disaster makes it clear that opposition to constitutional follies is not a question of strengthening the right but of sense, allowing the party – left and right – to do its job properly. The basic reforms are better listed:

Emancipate the parliamentary party
Restoring the confidence and independence of MPs is the first requirement even if many of the newer ones are now so programmed they don't want it. Best done by shifting the reselection balance from a mandatory system, which gives the MP a full-time job defending his back, to a voluntary basis. Reorganise the PLP, make the subject groups effective teams and give them a real role in formulating policies in conjunction with the front-bench spokesmen. In this way the PLP can develop its responses to the government and situations as things develop rather than expecting MPs to speak lines carved in stone by conference. It can also expand its own policy contribution to the party. No compromise is possible between internal and external party unless the internal party formulates policy proposals. There is a wealth of ability even in today's PLP. It must be mobilised. Real democracy demands that the PLP organise itself like the Australian or New Zealand caucus system as a prior-parliament.

Reorganise the national executive
By providing for automatic representation of councillors and the Parliamentary Labour Party in specific groups represented as of right. Prevent it from being a base for the internal opposition by providing that MPs can sit only in their own section, not in the reduced trade union and constituency section. Trade union representatives are best elected at conference and need a minimum attendance requirement to ensure they give it due and proper attention. Constituency representatives can be made more genuinely representative by being elected on a regional basis through regional conferences rather than the present method. This would give them a sense of responsibility by having to answer to an area.

Liberate the policy process
Conference should discuss what it is best at – broad general issues of the day, rather than detailed binding resolutions

passed after desultory discussion, usually without being understood. Policy can then be formulated through the broad assessments of the mood of the party as shown by these debates and by the passage of a drastically reduced number of resolutions selected on a rota basis from those which have come up through the regional conferences. The work of preparing policy should be done by combined meetings of the PLP subject groups and the NEC policy subcommittees, with the advice of experts, pollsters and advisors to widen the range of contributions. Their published recommendations, party green papers, should then be subject to discussion in both the Parliamentary Labour Party and the party conference, emerging as a white paper before going to a policy council of NEC and PLP representatives. This needs to be in continuous session, not just called before an election, and in continuous consultation with the shadow cabinet. Translating the emerging policies into the language of priorities, which is the mother tongue of socialism, must be the responsibility of a shadow cabinet which will have to implement them.

Broaden the base of membership
A shrinking party involvement in an age of mass leisure is inevitable. Yet it is particularly dangerous for a Labour Party taken over by unrepresentative activists. They have to be diluted by reaching out to new members through a reduced subscription and a two-tier membership, with associate members paying the kind of sum normally collected at flag days. It is possible in this way to give a huge boost to membership; the New Zealand Labour Party increased its membership tenfold, changing its whole character in the process. Associate membership could give an involvement in the party but no commitment to activity, and associates should receive regular mailing from the party nationally and locally. Full members will have the benefit of a direct involvement through postal ballot and postal primaries for the selection and reselection of MPs, councillors, party officials and such policy decisions as the choice of conference remits. Thus a GMC can be turned into a more genuinely representative body, running the party on behalf of a mass membership but

without the detailed participation. If it has proper digestion of business by the executive it can be freer for those general purposes and discussions, which are far more important than the boring reports and continuous diet of resolutions, minutiae and bickering most waste their time on now.

Revise the role of the trade unions

Ballast is vital for a party but not if it keeps shifting from side to side unpredictably. Nor should we take the same attitude to unions that Hindus do to cows. The role of the trade unions in the leadership electoral college should be reduced to 25 per cent, the same share as the constituencies, with the proviso that their leadership decisions shall be taken only on the basis of postal ballot of those members who pay the political levy. This will be difficult and expensive. Yet if the unions are not prepared to make the necessary effort they have no claim to participate. Similarly affiliation has to mean access by the Labour Party to those members who affiliate for mailing and local party purposes. The contributions of the union to the policy decision at conference should only be by block vote on those subjects where their members have been balloted by post. On all other votes their delegates should have a one-for-one weight with the constituency party representatives, such votes being regarded as 'policy suggestions' and not binding.

Change the nature of conference

It needs to be the pinnacle of a pyramid of regional conferences so that business can come to it predigested and prepared. At the moment the regional conferences of the Labour Party have no real role except as a sounding board. They need to be built up and integrated into the policy structure. MPs and candidates need the right to attend and vote on the same basis as constituency parties, so that they can give a lead and justify themselves instead of being a coconut shy.

Fix the frontier

The concomitant of a democratic party is control over those who can use it, to prevent abuse for purposes other than the party's. Effective differentiation between Labour and those socialist sects which will toil on forever at the lunatic end of the spectrum requires both a prescribed list, so that moving targets can be shot down, and a membership declaration which enshrines not Clause Four, as relevant now as the 39 Articles to the Church of England and twice as difficult to interpret, but a commitment to a socialist society along the lines of the statement of principles drawn up in 1960 affirming that the better society is achieved through parliamentary action and the leadership of the Parliamentary Labour Party. Such a statement will not stop deliberate deceit but it will allow abuses to be dealt with on a fair and rational basis instead of scratching round for pretexts.

Such changes strengthen the Labour Party as what it should be: a machine for winning elections and improving the lot of the people it represents. They widen it from the ideological debating society it has become, where cool consideration is replaced by party civil war, into a machine for winning. In each case strong vested interests are opposed. They will use their entrenched position. Yet parties too are subject to the dictates of evolution. If they are unable to change and evolve with the times they weaken themselves, decline and are gradually overtaken by the fate evolution holds in store for those who do not adjust. Labour is now in that situation. The activists have control and have to be persuaded to give it up. The trade unions dominate yet have to be persuaded to modify their power. The ideologues are entrenched but must be weakened. The internal preoccupation is paramount but it must be dissipated. In each case the change is harmful to those concerned but essential for the overall interests of the party. If they refuse to change the party is weakened and relegated to a position of permanent decline which takes them down with it.

One other change is less certainly beneficial and will excite even more opposition. It nevertheless needs to be considered. Proportional representation has become an anathema to the Labour Party without even being examined. This ill-considered instinctive rejection may disbar Labour from one possible way forward. A system which equates party allegiances in the electorate to shares of seats is the only

fair basis for democracy, so that it is curious that electoral
reform does not appeal to the party of democracy, particularly one which began by espousing proportional representation or, to give it its PR–conscious initials, PR, and has
never actually expunged that commitment but simply forgotten it and hidden the evidence in embarrassment.

The basic argument for proportional representation is that
it is fair and democratic. No one can build a democratic
superstructure on an undemocratic foundation. Labour
governments which have tried have found that this electoral
system in ages of instability or decline gives undue weight to
negative factors and protest votes. It becomes inherently
unstable, so that it is impossible to carry through any 'permanent and irreversible shift in the balance of power and wealth
to working people and their families.' In the 1960s and 1970s
progress was immediately reversible. In the 1980s reaction
looks to be enthroned. Surprisingly, these arguments have
not carried great conviction in Labour ranks. There has
always been the hope that it was Labour's turn next time and
the gambler's instinct has overcome rational calculation.

Now new factors have assumed greater importance. The
political system is now even more unbalanced. The emer-
gence of a multi-party system, whether called a 2.5 or a 2.23
party system, within the constrictions of a first-past-the-post
electoral system, which works well only with two dominant
parties, can produce some very curious results. It did in 1983
when it gave Mrs Thatcher a massive bonus in seats. The system demonstrably works in favour of a Conservative Party
which has a minority of votes yet gets an overwhelming
majority of seats because the forces opposed to it are
divided. Division on the left means rule on the right.

Now Labour has declined from being one of two dominant
parties, with all that that implies in terms of a vested interest
in the existing electoral system, to an under-party, something
between a major contender and a minority party. It is still
able to dream of power but less likely to get it and, on the
basis of the 1974–79 experience, less likely to get a governing
majority if it does. Such a situation requires Labour to take
a new look at its ingrained hostility to change in a system
which the country has now out grown. Labour must coolly

assess whether it is going to rise back to dominant status through its own efforts or whether it now needs to use the extra leverage available through espousing change in the electoral system.

With PR the whole orientation of a party is changed and Labour needs that change. The prospect of taking power, not through our own virtues, but through the failures of an incumbent Tory government, has put a premium on capturing power within the Labour Party so as to be in a position to dominate and control a Labour government when it is elected. Those days are passed with the stopping of the pendulum. PR, on the other hand, puts the emphasis on reaching out, talking to the electorate, to build up the basis of popular support which is the only true way to electoral victory. This is just the emphasis Labour needs to break out of its ghetto. PR also holds out the prospect of power for an under-party. The German Social Democrats are not a natural majority, though not as far fallen as us. Yet they have held power regularly since 1966 on the basis of coalitions. In the same way PR should allow Labour to escape from its relegation to the declining areas and interests to reach out, widening its appeal by giving the party in the great barren areas of the south the prospect of electing candidates. It would also allow Labour to form arrangements, allowing the nation's natural majority for altruism, welfare, public spending and social improvement to express itself electorally.

This immediately produces fears of coalition. Labour abhors coalition. Yet if coalition is the only way to get to power, then it is the responsibility of a party dedicated to improving the lot of the people, and to reversing the Thatcher disaster, to take it, not to nurture the purity of its misguided principles at the expense of misery for the people it represents. The exact form such a relationship will take is for us to decide. It could run a whole gamut from pact to full-blown coalition. The prospect of a referendum on proportional representation becomes a major negotiating counter with the Alliance, or more particularly with the Liberal wing of it, since on that basis they could be detached from the SDP. They may even come together with us to talk about mutual withdrawals of candidates to strengthen each other's chances in different parts of the country. With that electoral victory for the left next time rather than the time after that becomes a real possibility. All that it is necessary to concede in these negotiations is a referendum for PR, but even with PR eventually carried, as it certainly would be in a referendum, it would be wrong to assume that the Liberals will get in seats the same share they get now in votes. The vote now is a negative protest motivated by dislike of the other two parties, and last time particularly Labour. It is not any real enthusiasm for Liberalism. Under PR every vote is a wanted vote. The effects of that vote on government have to be considered. Thus the blend of pious impracticalities and populist impossibilities which the Liberals now offer would be distinctly less attractive. Their support would not fall to the level of the Free Democrats in Germany, who last time only just surmounted the 5 per cent threshold. Yet it would certainly be lower than it is now.

The perverse relationship between seats and votes demonstrated in 1983 has created a strong vested interest in the first-past-the-post electoral system. That interest is stronger in the Conservative Party, where crime has clearly paid, than in the ranks of Labour: even on a straight transfer of vote shares to seat shares we are only twenty-nine up. The chief gainers would be the Alliance with 160 seats; the real losers the Conservatives, 111 down. No one can provide strong government by disfranchising huge numbers, and Labour is dedicated to fairness. We cannot now escape its obligations by an unthinking attachment to a dogma about a first-past-the-post system which has so demonstrably failed to serve us. There are those who argue that we should cling to it as the only thing which keeps Labour viable. Such a view is nonsense. Nothing can keep an irrelevant party going for ever, but we have only been reduced to danger level by our internal preoccupation which the present electoral system has fostered. Labour must think about PR as part of a concern with its own situation and its own future. That does not mean instant conversion; change only comes slowly in a party like ours. It really means being aware of the benefits PR can hold out and realising that we are not going to achieve power at one stride. We run the electoral race with a big ball and chain on one foot, and that the left. Awareness that first-past-the-post can handicap, coupled with a sense of our responsibility to our people and to the country, should prepare us not to bow at the knee before proportional representation but to recognise, like an aging sex enthusiast, that aids previously thought inconceivable may now be necessary. One of them is the possibility for a new deal and new stepping-stones to power that a willingness to negotiate about PR can bring to a Labour Party which may otherwise be relegated to permanent opposition.

The choice is between realism and nurturing our dreams in what will be impotence and could well be decline. For practical politicians the choice is simple: Labour's responsibility is to take power and stop the Thatcher counter-revolution at the first opportunity. Any government in which Labour is the dominant element, even a Labour government without a brain in its head or a policy in its manifesto, would be better for the mass of British people than a Tory government compounding all the adverse economic trends and then using decline as the excuse to cut back spending and so making things worse again. Any way to secure such a government – PR, deals, a referendum – is not only legitimate but a matter of duty. The main voice against it will be the ideologues who have reduced the party to this position in the first place. The warning is of general relevance. Labour has been reduced by its own follies to a situation where it is perilously poised between a march back to power, which must be slow, requiring more than one election, and further slippage, not towards the abyss but towards that ghetto of dwindling support, dying enthusiasm, to which parties which have ceased to move with the people and the times crawl away to die. Too many mistakes have been too disastrous to make more and get away with it. Only drastic changes will save the party. If those changes are resisted in a defence of entrenched vested interests then the public will be unforgiving because Labour will have opted for irrelevance. Which is why the changes have to be made, however great the difficulties, however great the risk of restarting all that divisive process of discussion and argument which has been so much strengthened in the last four years. The first requirement is clear-headedness: an accurate judgement on the party's situation, the near-trad-gedy which has engulfed it and its causes in the four years which went before. The 1983 election is an appalling warning to a party which has shown itself capable of ignoring all the auguries and warnings up to now.

9 · Talking with the People

Time and again the Labour Party has been elected to power and tried to implement capitalist policies better than the Tories. We want to see no more of that . . . No more must we go into power with the proviso that we try to make workers pay for the crisis of Capitalism.

ARTHUR SCARGILL

Policy was Labour's main problem in the ostrich years. It is today. The basic failure then was not to recognise what policy is. Labour approached it in mechanical fashion, developing policy through set, and largely unsuitable, procedures, as an expression of the will of the party, or rather the section which happened to be dominant. The products were imposed on the rest of the party, including a leadership which had been espousing something different for years, or compromised with them. It was then set out in a shopping list, the bigger the more relevant, and presented to the electorate on a take-it-or-leave-it basis. Love me, love my policy. They didn't particularly like either.

This mechanistic view of policy contrasts sharply with the Tory view. Policy formulation for them is a branch of public relations; people pleasing, not perfection producing, devising by alchemy a policy designed more for its appeal than for its effect: cut taxes without saying how; bring law and order by hints of toughness rather than changes in society; say what people want rather than what they are likely to get and don't agonise too much about the consequences. Expecting Tory promises to be fulfilled in power is rather like being lured into a massage parlour and getting a massage. Labour could never be like that. Yet the ideologues who argue that to be so is the only alternative to resolutionary socialism are wrong. There is sense.

Policy is a blend of three elements combined to make it a process of communication, the language in which party talks with people about their common problems and the community they want to shape together, rather than a route map for getting there. It develops a common instinct to move forward, providing a guide to the steps that have to be taken. It is the language of values and aspirations, not detailed prescriptions which fade with fashion and date with time. Early Labour aspirations for a better society, mankind elevated above the daily struggle, remain today as fresh as in the 1900s. Yet the 1983 bumper-bundle will soon fall apart in the dustbin of history.

The first element is the party itself. In policy it expresses its personality; assertive and hectoring in 1983, talking at people rather than to them; simple and confident in 1945. What Labour should be expressing is that it is a party about people, aspiring to make a better life for them. It puts them first, over and above the interests of the few, over immutable economic laws, over the power of wealth and institutions or classes; and the prescriptions are not ideology but the values of caring, sharing, working together for equality and progress. It takes a genius for malcommunication to allow such noble sentiments to be maligned as a brutish desire to domineer, requiring a New Budapest to be builded here in England's green and pleasant land.

The second contributory is the problem. Britain's are those of decline. The system cannot now support the superstructure. Despite the oil the disaster can only get worse since in a world of intense competition, growth begets growth, decline begets decline. Britain is on its way downhill to a divided society with a permanent level of high unemployment and a shrinking industrial base unable to provide growth, bear taxation or pay her way in the world. Unless that problem is tackled the whole panoply of welfare, public spending and improvement which we have built up so slowly since the war cannot even survive, let alone be updated to the levels common in competitor countries. A crumbling welfare state sits on sinking foundations.

Third element in the equation is the market for the product; the people. The people's party has certain real disadvantages here. It assumes, because it springs from the people, that it knows them. It doesn't. The only way is to listen, to pause and to communicate with the people and to call in the new world of the polls and panels, to redress the incoherence of the old. That costs money and sacrifices pride.

The society to which we respond is more sophisticated, better educated, more pluralistic. It is neither libertarian nor radical, indeed strangely conservative compared with more pragmatic societies in Anglo-Saxon democracies and in more ideological electorates in Europe. It still has to be approached in broad general terms as one nation in a tight little island, not as a series of subcultures, for they all have too little allegiance from the members they claim to represent; the party of the trade unions should know that. Britain still breathes, laughs, sighs and cheers as one nation, as viewers, consumers, at work, school, in sickness and in health. A party which aspires to represent them must address them as one.

What is this Britain which seems to have changed beyond our ken? Sociologically it is more middle class. Between 1979 and 1983 there was an increase of 5 per cent in the advertisers' categories A, B and C1, a corresponding decline in the skilled (−2 per cent) and the unskilled (−3 per cent) sections, a four-year embodiment of a long-sustained trend. Workers are more likely to be employed in services, and particularly public services, and white-collar jobs. Society is better off, better educated, more middle class, or at least classless, in the sense that it has more consumer durables, more likely to own its home − as six out of ten now do − to have a car and telephone and all things that make puritanical socialists uneasy, to have more leisure, even to take more holidays: things which were luxuries to Labour MPs and older party members as they grew up are inevitable parts of life. The money economy becomes more important, the managed economy rather less. Public sector monoliths and the machinery created to protect and help a dependent working class no longer look as benign. They can do more for

themselves and don't like being condescended to as society's
lame dogs because that isn't how they see themselves.

Labour's mistake has been not to move up with its people.
The skilled workers who started the party are now outside it,
a new middle class, but with preoccupations more selfish or
more practical than those of the solid middle class or even
the lower middle of old. They want a better life, a better
home, a better car, more money, a future for their children.
When it comes to values the British affirm Mrs Thatcher's:
health first, then family life and law and order, in that order
with entertainment and holidays well below love, money, job
satisfaction and neighbourhood. Sex is almost as badly
esteemed as politics. Non-material things are highly rated,
and the striking characteristic of the British is the poverty of
their imagination. The poorest in Europe, they are the most
satisfied with their lot. There is no vaulting ambition for
themselves or their country. All the surveys indicate not only
a low level of ambition but the crucial importance of the
money flow, take home pay and the total coming into the
household in all forms, benefits accepted as a right, wife's
wages taken as given, husband's earnings and the savings
from that growing counterpart of domestic service of yore,
the DIY and the black, or more accurately the 'household',
economy.

Their aspirations for their country are as low as for themselves. They are proud of it and resentful of the greater
affluence and power of others, but prone to blame failure on
themselves, to accept it as inevitable, a national inferiority
complex which is replacing decades of superiority. They
don't particulary want greatness and are now reluctant to
have it thrust upon them: happy for the British government
to sit at a top table which they like to think is its right, but
not particularly prepared to do anything to keep it there.
This is a foreign policy perfectly compatible with the status of
a third-rank power to which Britain has now sunk.

To combine these three elements, party, problems,
people, is the essence of Labour's difficulties. We have not
done so. Problem and people are the real incompatibilities.
The public does not realise, let alone understand, what is
happening and is unprepared to envisage the measures

necessary to cope with it. Yet the people are pragmatic, as immune to Tory doctrinaires as to our own. If the state has to act to protect a community which realises that it is threatened then common sense will accept it. It rejects the doctrinaire such as nationalisation, *dirigisme* and controls, the building of great monoliths and the equally doctrinaire insistence that it is better to do nothing than have it done by the state is just as firmly ruled out. The obvious it will accept, provided it has confidence in the people saying it. People and practical approaches they can be persuaded to accept but not assertion and ideology merchandised by obvious incompetents.

Appealing to this new majority is now a matter of strategy. The submerged fifth remains, still identifying with Labour and describing itself as 'working class', still characterised by low pay, bad conditions, real basic needs, living in council houses, concentrated in the older industrial areas. Yet it is a smaller proportion of the population, an insufficient base from which to build a majority. Labour must reach out into the new majority. The improvement in their life-style, the dynamics of a mass consumer society and the mass media have caused the new middle class to identify upwards, thinking of themselves as the norm, the poor and unemployed as the exception. They concentrate on their own situation and draw apart. This is not a sell-out to selfishness but human nature. Labour must show them where their real interest lies, emphasising that it certainly is not best served by an identification with highly concentrated wealth, power and privilege of which they have, by voting Conservative, constituted themselves the front line. In doing so Labour is talking to the country as a whole. This new middle class is the new majority, the essence of a nation which is increasingly living in the south-east, working in the tertiary sector and doing jobs using educationally derived skills. Labour can offer them far more than the Conservatives, provided it talks to them in relevant language, concentrates on the quality of life as well as basics and makes the connections clear. It is still their natural ally. In financial terms their interests lie with public spending and common provision of services: health, education, child benefit, retirement. They are the section of society which suffers most from protective monopolies which flourish in the fields into which they are now venturing: lawyers, estate agents, the uncertainties of insurance and accident compensation, exhorbitant interest rates and the practices of fringe banking, private loans, and hire purchase, the lack of genuine competition between banks and among building societies, the fiddles of pension schemes and their transfers, the inadequacies of consumer protection on major purchases. Their interest is in expansion which improves their incomes and the market for their skills and the prospects for their children, provided it is a reasonable expansion, not a bursting bubble which threatens what they have. They also suffer, though not like the unemployed, when the economy is run down. Thus Labour's role as protector of the people against abuse and entrenched privilege is directly relevant to them. Thatchernomics, putting the interests of money and those who have, or, manipulate it, above the interests of people and those who make things, is directly harmful. The new middle class are borrowers, the victims of the high interests rates and crippling mortgages which result directly from monetarist economics. They need a more progressive tax system and instead of the grudging help of state monoliths they want the backing and the provision to allow them to help themselves, by bringing power to influence their own lives closer to them, by decentralisation and division of power, by offering help for them and the pressure and interest groups they form. Conservatives want them deferential and grateful. Labour wants them standing on their own two feet, as bolshy and self-interested as they can be at work and as they were when they formed the Labour Party to improve themselves.

Prescribing the groups does not dictate the policy. Labour needs to develop broad relevant policies and then emphasise the benefits they offer to the groups to be won: broadcasting, not narrowcasting. The skills are those of the analyst, the specialist, the blender and the salesman. Nowhere is the ideologue relevant. Nor indeed is the political theorist. Much as Labour needs an updating of Anthony Crosland's *Future of Socialism*, policy formulation is nothing like as fundamental – we need an identity, not a theory. The theoretical basis

will come after a successful Labour government as Crosland's own did. It is not the indispensible prelude.

The other area to be avoided is that of discussing socialism. It is a perennial problem in a Labour Party where everything has to be discussed in socialist terms. Yet definitions
vary and discussion is often pointless because it starts from
different angles and produces no meeting of minds. The
essence of socialism is a society based on liberty, equality and
fraternity, in which the economic power of individuals,
classes and institutions is harnessed for the common good
through democratic control of the economic resources of that
community. That is all we need. No need to wander off into
statism or foist the whole business on to the public. To be
constantly talking about 'socialism' and policies as 'socialist'
is to cut ourselves off. It is our language and our aspiration.
It is not that of the mass of the people and we should be talking to them, not to each other.

There are no miracle policies, undiscovered answers, striking solutions. All that is available is a different blend, a new
shuffling of the pack and a new tone and emphasis. What
Labour needs is a public stance, a perceived identity, not the
ability to cross every t. Margaret Thatcher projected herself
as the voice of the new majority by voicing its populist
attitudes: anti-big government, pro-freedom, competition,
profit and getting on. Labour now needs its own populism
instead of cart loads of ideology; altruism and concern
because they are widespread; improving and advancing
because that is what people want; helping rather than providing because that is the stage they are at; all leavened with a
touch of nationalism because there is national economic
strength to be rebuilt and populism to be turned against fat
cats and the financial interests who ride on the backs of the
middle people. Community and togetherness too. People
want them and they are now an economic reality: we get on
together or not at all. The poverty of seven million, the
unemployment of four, weaken us all, make us all poorer.

Labour needs to turn from a defensive party protecting
and cossetting to a buoyant party of progress. Expansion is
the key. Let's grow with Labour. The consequences of
decline are draconian and fascist. Its sacrifices fall on the

people. It divides and embitters. It turns people against each other. Britain still needs hope, if not *New Hope*.

The mood can only be changed by the gentle buoyancy which comes from expansion, stimulating investment, spreading good cheer, making the whole community better off by putting people back to work and resources back to use. It is still possible, given North Sea oil, provided it is made a central commitment of government as Mrs Thatcher did with inflation. The techniques are not those of eastern Europe but using the forces of the market to the maximum. The state, natural protector of the people, can do more by creating the climate, setting the stage for growth and providing the incentives and the fuel, than it can by a detailed interference it is neither fitted for nor competent to do. The state is ringmaster, not act. Its basic function is to prod and persuade. We have the least enterprising capitalists, the least risk-taking capital, the least dynamic business and the least innovative management in the world. A state's boot up the backside is needed to change these attitudes, to stimulate and drive forward. What it achieves will be in partnership, not by control or domination.

Expansion requires effective control of finance, making money the servant of the people, not their master, taking the necessary power to use finance for the wider interest by making the Bank of England an agent of policy, not a fifth column for finance, manipulating government for the purposes of the City. Appointing a minister as governor is not a long step from appointing the prime minister's friends. It would ensure that cabinet's wishes were followed and allow the government to reassert its control of interest rates instead of leaving them to a market which is managed anyway.

A new Industrial Reorganisation Corporation and an investment bank will be necessary to provide long-term low interest rate, loans and to act as the public merchant banker. A new public competitor on the high streets, formed from the amalgamation of the TSB, the Giro and the NSB, would propel the banking system to expansion, low interest rates and finance for investment. The central problem of the British economy has always been the dominance of finance which has imposed a stultifying climate of conservatism on industry, shackling it by high interest rates and an obsession with short-term profitability and balance sheet considerations.

The basis of 1983's plan for rebuilding the economy was the Alternative Economic Strategy: import controls, planning agreements and centralised planning. The economic situation will get worse and as it does the AES may become more relevant, yet not fast enough to make it politically acceptable or even practicable. The alternative is to insulate and stimulate, not by a *dirigisme* which hardens arteries, but by a competitive currency. Government controls the exchange rate through the level of interest rates. Most of the damage done to industry and employment has been done by the unprecedented rise in the exchange rate from 1977 onwards. While we have oil as an overdraft facility we can still reverse this and rebuild, throwing the dynamics into reverse by bringing down the pound and keeping it competitive. This boosts the most crucial industries, the internationally traded sector by stimulating exports, penalising imports. The market can do more, more quickly, more flexibly and more cheaply than controls working with capitalism and stimulating by a deliberate policy of cheap money.

Britain's problem is production. Unless we rebuild production nothing else is possible. The first priority is rebuilding a shattered economy before we can rebuild a shattered welfare state. For the consumer side of Labour's strategy the timetable is longer. A Labour Party which pledges benefits and increases more than the economy can obviously afford, as we did in 1983, or which rushes in to expand benefits and spending before the economy has grown enough to finance them, as we did in 1974, is neither credible nor competent. Our image as the party of improved benefits and welfare is strong enough to sustain us but we do need to offer a few big broad benefits for electoral appeal. The problem is to humanise a welfare state seen as a grudging dole, to make it a welfare community and to concentrate on benefits and changes which are both attractive and a stimulus to expansion. In administration we need the Bill Rodgers formula: maximum effect for minimum expenditure. Concentrating resources where they can do most good, and cutting down bloated bureaucracies to personalise the system, is realistic.

Wealth is best created by a society to which all contribute: an equal society is an efficient society. This requires both a change of attitudes and better directed spending, changing the tax system to stop it being a middle-class benefit system and make it genuinely progressive, spreading the burden fairly and advancing a more equal society. This means widening the tax base by cutting back the undergrowth of exemptions and allowances which, over the years, have taken more and more income out of taxation, then with a genuine capital gains tax bringing inflationary gains back into the net, a restored structure of capital taxes and a wealth tax levying fortunes over £100,000, the progressive tax structure can create a sharper gap of self-interest between those who are beneficiaries, Labour's natural voters, and those who carry the burdens because they are better able to do so.

The march of equality is not an advance to a uniform society but rather based on the Rawlsian principle that every inequality must be justified. This principle appeals to a population which would not know the difference between Rawls and a plug in the wall yet has a strong levelling instinct and a feeling for fairness in hard times. Fairness is achieved through the tax system and a national strategy for incomes. Incomes policy is necessary to cope with the inflationary consequences of expansion. It is socially fair and allows a more rapid reduction of unemployment than would otherwise be possible. It is popular provided it is seen to be fair. The next step is breaking down the entrenched privileges of protectionist interest groups, starting with the most powerful: the legal profession, its pay, perks and privileges; the farmers, the sacred cow of the British economy with rating relief like other religions and the highest *per capita* recipients of state support in Britain; the medical and accountancy professions, the estate agents, the finance sector. All have been quick to lecture the rest of the economy on competitiveness and dynamism. All will want to encourage both processes by setting an example.

Liberty, equality, and fraternity are principles of social organisation as well as Labour's central slogans. Liberty because a firm base must be provided in the basic needs for homes, jobs and benefits for the rest of the people to pursue their own rights and interests through the framework provided by the community. Equality comes through making every privilege justify itself. Fraternity is the welfare society; the community in action to bring help where it is needed the most, in the most direct fashion and without the intervention of the huge monoliths which now depersonalise it.

The principles are not in themselves sufficient. Populist instincts we have viewed with suspicion: somehow unworthy; not right or proper for an idealistic party. We need to harness and channel them for better purposes; nationalism and patriotism as a drive for rebuilding a powerful British economy which can be a source of wealth, improvement and national pride; populism as an instinct against monoliths and entrenched vested interests and both against the Common Market. Separation is essential to rebuild our economy. There is no need to prejudge every issue and provide for every contingency by saying what we would do in hypothetical situations. Anglo-Gaullism should govern our approach to the EEC, national assertiveness, mobilising popular dislike for national purposes more courageously than Mrs Thatcher who has only done it for cash. The central national purpose is British industry. We must take power to make our own decisions by repealing Section 2 of the European Communities Act and then subjecting each aspect of membership to scrutiny, putting a tariff on manufactured imports, buying food cheaply elsewhere and moving on in an escalation which will lead logically to withdrawal but arrive there by a popular route, not the shock of anticipation. Until then much market as suits our interests, as little as we can get away with.

The same philosophy holds in defence. Abandoning British nuclear weapons was unacceptable to an electorate which did not want more American missiles and would not face the expense of updating the British delivery system. Labour offered more to anti-nuclear opinion that any other party: no Trident, no Cruise. It made no sense to go the whole hog and offer to be nuclear free too. Far more sensible (and popular) to put the aging Polaris system and Britain's other nuclear weapons into negotiation, keeping them if those negotiations do not succeed. Like a baby with a dummy, the British and French electorates prefer the comfort of nuclear defence which will never be used and which they can't afford to update.

The public wants to remain part of the NATO alliance. So does Labour. We only have influence in American counsels through it. It gives defence on the cheap by sharing effort and allowing specialisation. Yet it also implies maintaining a nuclear commitment on bases which have been there throughout the post-war period. The bases, the delivery system and the planes will soon be outdated. Better, therefore, to maintain good relations and let sleeping dogs lie.

The final triumph of patriotism is a full-scale attack on the Thatcher administration which is possible for an opposition which has an alternative, confidence in it and which has been proved right. As long as there was the possibility that policies of discipline and deflation in which the public half believed might work, the popular instinct was to give them a go: Labour was asking people to say in advance that the sacrifices which they had made, many of them willingly because people quite like discipline for other people, were not going to work. It was unreasonable to expect it. Yet in a short time the disaster will be perfectly clear. Mrs Thatcher's time is running out. Her government will be forced either into a humiliating reversal or into persevering in discipline and depression which are seen to be harmful and known not to work. Meanwhile the rest of the world, lesser breeds without the oil, will be growing prosperous by not doing what the British government has been doing. Every day will make it clearer that a government which has invoked patriotism is ruining the nation it claims to be strengthening. It will become glaringly apparent that the only obstacle to rebuilding Britain, to using the brief and contracting opportunity which oil provides, will be the Thatcher government itself. By laying the ground for that turn of the tide now, reinforcing the arguments against what has been done, rather than putting forward our own distracting alternatives, by exuding a natural and real confidence that things do not have to be this way, Labour will stand ready to seize the moment. It will be able to mobilise a broad coalition of national anger against the government. Instead of confusing the issue with talk of socialism or a code language understood only by ourselves, we must address the obstacle in the only language to which an angry public will respond: 'You have been here too long for any good that you have been doing. Begone and let us have done with you in the name of God, go.'

10 · From *New Hope* to New Life

The right-wing reformists have seen the collapse of their policies. The policies of all the tendencies of Tribune, and of the left reformists, are utopian. That is why the ideas of Marxism which are based on the objective realities and the economic processes of capitalism are winning more and more support within the rank and file Labour movement. The working class has no other way out than the road of socialism.

MILITANT

Smothered in all their hucksterism and their hysteria, elections are at bottom a serious choice: a decision on how the country has been run for the last few years, an indication of what the electorate expects for the future. In 1983 that choice was more momentous than most, between a government whose policies were compounding decline and an opposition desperate to rebuild and reconstruct. The electorate not only declined to make, or even to see, the choice, it rebuked the opposition. Thanks to Labour's previous behaviour a great opportunity was reduced to an irrelevance. A government whose policies had already failed was returned to office with a mandate to do its worst. An opposition whose policies were not without risk and uncertainy but which were still the only way of fighting back against decline was relegated and enfeebled while the two-party system, great engine of democratic change, was weakened and undermined. That was the outcome of four years hard Labour.

The Conservative Party had fought one war, three thousand miles away and done well out of it. Labour had fought a civil war, a power struggle within the party, which turned

Labour's whole attention inwards. It was seen as a left–right argument. Yet this was mere label-trading for constitutional changes and power struggles are ideologically neutral. Whoever wins is subject to the same tight constraints of public opinion and party role as those they replace. It is therefore useless to apportion blame between those who made the changes and those who resisted them. Both combined to produce a self-absorption which cut Labour off from power.

Thus this story is four years in the death of a party which cut itself off from the real world. All parties have an internal life: they are big, complex organisations. If that internal life becomes more obsessive than the real world in which the party has to operate then it incapacitates itself, as much use as a car whose engine produces more banging and flames than power. To change images from the metaphysical one of the title to the more realistically mechanical, is Labour's vehicle now at the end of its useful life, as it sits steaming by the roadside? Or with the benefit of whatever mechanical changes are possible, an engine rebuild or more likely a quick tinker, plus a bit of downhill running, will it get back on the road and fulfil its purpose?

This is a 'whither Labour' question of the type asked in an outpouring of studies. None saw that it is really two questions, one about the party and one about its prospects. Road conditions first. The going should get easier. Winners take on an added aura, Harold Wilson in 1966, Margaret Thatcher today. Yet those who live by the media die by them and the prime minister is distinctly pregnable. The chickens are not only coming home to roost in the form of spending cuts, rising interest rates and rising unemployment, but her post-dated cheque comes up for presentation and the policies cannot work. No strategy for fighting inflation can succeed if it breaks it by depression and unemployment: the disciplines harm and once imposed cannot be taken off. The idea that low inflation brings revival is not true: it brings only the semi-retired economy for growth has to be worked, planned, organised and invested for. In a world where other countries do all those things and we don't, low inflation means only undignified decline. No strategy for incentives can work if it involves an increasing burden of taxation pressing on a shrinking productive base. No strategy for competitiveness works if it depends on management by money. A high pound and high interest rates ruin the industry which provides the jobs, the surplus for spending and the ability to survive in a world growing colder and harder.

Britain and her government now survive only through oil and asset sales. Both will have a dwindling impact: the oil has peaked and what public investments can be sold to keep down borrowing are fast going, going, gone. So government comes up against fundamental dilemmas: increase taxes or cut benefits and spending; increase spending in counter-cyclical fashion or endure deepening depression; cut imports by more deflation or see the balance of payments slide into disaster.

Nemesis waits. Seeing that is neither a matter of predictive powers nor leaked cabinet papers but common sense. Just as surely as 1961, the year of squeeze, freeze and deflation, followed from Harold Macmillan's 1959, so 1985 (or 1986, the anniversary of Labour's IMF debacle) will be the inevitable consequence of Margaret Thatcher's 1983. Disaster when it strikes will be bigger and harder because this wastrel government has been more spendthrift and short-sighted. It has thrown away the oil and Britain's last chance with it.

When Nemesis comes can Labour be far behind? The answer must be equivocal. We are already far behind: a decline which has gone so far must make recovery more than a one-stage process. The shackles which caused the problems in the first place are fastened hard and any attempt to take them off will cause further controversy and bitterness of the type which has done so much harm already. Decline is self-reinforcing, for being relegated to declining areas, sectors, membership and connections means greater insulation from reality, a hardening in the mould. The third party which tripped up Labour in 1983 will still be there to provide the same service for a reviving one. The Liberals could sidetrack discontent again and will have better prospects in by-elections than a general election. The SDP now has post-electoral *triste* but whether as a separate party or as an afterthought tagged on to the Liberals, like the *Nation* to the *New Statesman*, it will hover over Labour like a vulture, ready to pounce on its weakness and benefit from its mistakes.

The shock of defeat has not produced a sudden, clear vision from those blind enough to have stumbled into such disasters in the first place. Even if it did, where is the leverage for change to come from? Ten million monkeys with ten million block votes could not reconstruct the folly of Labour's national executive, able at any moment to drift away to insanity, undermining any beneficial changes which may be initiated. The trade unions have the power from outside but are too divided, lack the common will to intervene and do not command their own organisations for such a purpose. They must in any case come to terms with the government. Labour's decline as a viable instrument will accelerate this so that, given a modicum of ministerial cunning, their interest in saving the party will never again be as great as it was in 1983. Even then they could really help only with money. So Labour is deadlocked. The party cannot be brought into a sensible stand-off relationship with the unions while the left controls constituencies and machine. It cannot be saved from a left whose impact has been disastrous without the union. The only balancing force, the PLP, is not now a party but two blocks, their weights falling unevenly into the different scales.

The constitutional problem is complicated by the balance of power between left and right which cuts across it. Labour is always and inevitably divided between left and right. Each needs the other, the left providing the dynamic and the principle, the right public acceptability and a sense of realism. Since both are essential neither can dominate and exclude the other from power. The condition of progress is that they live and work together in fraternity, or as much of it as is possible where strong feelings hold sway. Up to the 1970s they have coexisted. Not so from 1979–83. The right was discredited by government, the left restive, pushed forward by forces it only half understood. The changed balance of power could not be accommodated in the old *modus vivendi* and lack of trust and a need for symbolic victories required that it be written into the constitution, a process the right was bound to resist. For its part the triumphant left failed to understand the responsibilities of a major party in a two-party system and was incompetent in its appeal to the public. After long years of opposition it was depressingly negative in its approach. It spoke the language of ideology, not the people and had no higher enemy than those in its own party: once they were beaten it had all too little idea of what to do next.

The new skippers did not know how to run the ship and despised the arts by which their predecessors had done so. Meanwhile the inevitable reaction of the right compounded the problem. No longer in control, they were rather like a team of aging opera singers who found themselves fronting a rock show. They didn't like the job. And it showed. Thus the basic benefit of coalition, as a teaching device showing groups how to get on so that they can better get on with the real world, was frustrated. Too little trust internally meant too little ability to reach the people. Thus Labour was in no real condition to fulfil the requirements a two-party system imposes on its incumbents: to rally support, to become broad coalition against the party in power, to conciliate support by broad lowest common denominator policies, to look out rather than in. This might not have mattered had the promised radicalisation of the working class come like cavalry to the aid of the left's Custer when the Indians were found to be inconsiderately hostile. It did not. The public, bemused by the arguments and expecting an alternative, not a saloon bar brawling, turned away. Instead of having an alternative explained to them they were hectored by a discordant chorus, offering assertion, 'socialism' and an ideology which they did not understand. They came to the conclusion that Labour, their natural choice as an alternative only months before, was not now fit to govern.

The essential condition of progress, a new *modus vivendi* within the party, is less difficult to reach than outsiders believe. Things were settling down well before the election and provided there is no renewed power struggle there is an instinctive solidarity and loyalty within the party. Provided too the lessons of the election are clear. The dependence of the party on the public standing of the right was clearly revealed. So was the need to stay in touch with the public. A party seen to be left-dominated with a policy clearly more radical than ever before will not make progress. The leader needs to be the mediator between party and public. The right needs to be enrolled enthusiastically behind the policies; its popularity and presentational skills are essential. There is little point in concessions to the wilder shores of leftism: they have no other way to vote but Labour. The language of ideology produces total failure of communication with an electorate whose interests and preoccupations are very different. Provided these lessons are learned, provided most important of all the groups within the party can settle down together as they did from 1982 onwards, neither dominating, Labour is ready to move forward. If both address themselves to the real problems of policy and communion with the nation, rather than concentrating on each other, they can. The party is more important than its parts. Its mission is more vital than internal victories and defeats.

The basic problem all must face is one of responsibility. To whom is the party ultimately responsible? To the people? In which case how can their influence be brought to bear before despair reaches the point at which they have no alternative but that of humiliating a party which has erred and strayed from their ways? Or is Labour responsible to something less amorphous, more self-contained: the members, the movement or the working class? In which case why is membership shrinking and unrepresentative, why can't the movement deliver or the working class come home again? The answer is and must be the people, the source of power without which all else is futility. Yet rather than face this fundamental problem, Labour threw itself into the much more exciting, but slightly less relevant, issue of where should power lie in the party. Those who framed the constitution, like those who ran the party up to the 1970s, had wisely dodged this by letting the parliamentary party address itself to the people and giving it independence to do so, keeping the party for the movement. Social change, eroding the working-class base and creating new subcultures, coupled with the more frenetic politics of decline, forced the issue to the fore again. In attempting to face it, Labour entered a period of introspection, the political equivalent not of navel contemplation but of masturbation.

In a complex organisation truth is rarely pure and in the Labour Party it is never simple. The fundamental problems of responsibility and balance within the party will not be solved by any clear-cut decision either way. The solution is not to hope or try for total reconstruction of the organisation in the hope of making it relevant to a new age: that is desirable but given the inertia of a naturally conservative party, whose constitution is deadlocked, it may be impossible. It is to shift the emphasis, modifying the changes where possible, but changing the whole ethos of the party. The last four years have looked to the second side of the equation. The next four must look to the first, forcing us to turn our gaze outward, to adjust back to the people to whom we are responsible, even if they seem not to know it. Constitutional reform is not now crucial. The Bennite programme had run out of steam and out of widely agreed objectives. There is even the possibility of rolling back, modifying the reforms to make them work more efficiently, rather than seeking to reverse them. The real problem is policy. There the same procedures repeated will produce the same mistakes. Conference has no ability to determine priorities or moderate demands in the light of practicality, the outside party no incentive to do so, and the PLP, as yet, no will. The ritual slaughter of infant policies is not the most popular of strategies.

Nevertheless the emphasis in policy has to be switched from looking at party aspirations to reaching out to the wider community and channelling its attitudes and aspirations into the process. The strategic requirement is some reconciliation with the middle class, meaning both the middle class radicalism of old and the more pragmatic instincts of the new middle class. The greatest task in British politics is to effect a reconciliation between the two blocks of opinion opposed to the government: trade unions stultifying with Labour, and the more liberal of the old and new middle class, their instincts for welfare, altruism, concern and change pursued with diminishing enthusiasm through Labour or becalmed with the Alliance. In days of yore before the days of gore both were more radical, now they have become more selfish, the trade unions more negative, the reformers less likely to support change that hurts them. They were also once united in the Labour Party for each was essential to the other. Now they have fallen apart, reducing the anti-Tory side of politics to impotence. The key to victory is to bring them back together, preferably in the same party or alternatively in a working relationship between the different organisations to which each gives its allegiance.

If they combine their efforts they can throw out a Tory government and resume the politics of betterment and reform. This government has already shown that it will be as reactionary, as prejudiced and as incompetent, even as cruel, as it is allowed. Having allowed it in good measure by weakening ourselves, the only way to stop it now is either by reaching out to unite the broad coalition of votes which alone can defeat the government or restitching the old alliance together by other means.

The second is easier than the first, involving only the conquest of old enmities and old party prejudices against working arrangements with other parties. The first requires a determined and clear-headed effort to break out of the ghetto of decline, to shed sectarian attitudes by changing course and to rebuild. The party's instinct will be for the first, regarding the second as an abdication. Yet it is no use embarking on it without a clear-headed determination and the ability to carry it through. Both depend on Labour's own efforts. Labour now holds its fate in its own hands and the country's with it.

Prescription is easy. Yet Labour has already shown itself amazingly resistant to good advice, even obvious common sense. Now the problem of rationality is compounded by that of deadlocked authority and the self-reinforcing syndrome of decline. Prophecy is impossible. At every stage of the downhill slide optimistic ones were invalidated. Yet Thatcherite hubris must be followed by Tory Nemesis. When it does Labour's chance comes and the whole mood of politics alters. This could rescue Labour as it has before, transforming attitudes, distracting attention from problems, giving the party what it most needs, a sense of élan and movement, instead of floundering around in the doldrums with no idea

what to do. The tragedies of the last four years would have
been impossible in a party in which a sense of opportunity
sustained a feeling of confidence. The moods of politics do
not last forever, the Thatcher triumph rests on crumbling
foundations and the opportunities of change are enormous
with an increasingly volatile electorate. Within the space of
the last four years first Labour, then the Alliance, then, in
the Falklands war, the Conservatives each had around half
the popular preferences, reducing the other two parties to a
scrabble for the rest. Being in power the Conservatives had
the advantage of being able to end the game while they were
ahead yet now the game restarts, the government has used
up much of its room for manoeuvre with the economy and a
multi-party system, combined with an increasingly volatile
electorate, will make both snakes and ladders even more
abrupt.

That provides hope for Labour but also enormous risks.
There is now no leeway for the kind of mistakes Labour
made so liberally from 1979–83. Instead of putting the heat
on the government we made ourselves an issue. Instead of
presenting an impression of benign competence we rushed to
buy support and divided it by multiplying commitments.
Instead of working with the grain we rubbed against it.
Instead of countering the prime minister's schoolmarm lectures with warmth and humanity we offered only hectoring
ideology, striving to be a new product where people wanted
old certainties. Instead of moving into the centre ground
which government was vacating we moved to our own
extremes, unaware that Tory extremism is popular because
its language is that of populism, ours unacceptable because it
is ideological. A party which aspires to change the system
must work within it but we preferred gesture politics, demon-
strating our virility by taking on the system: providing ammunition by the ton for the world's most malign media, telling
the people that we wanted them to have, rather than listening, pretending that the third party would go away because
we wanted it to. We were prisoners of our own misconcep-
tions.

To move forward now we have only to abandon them and
live in the real world, not our ghetto. Logically it should not

be difficult. If we can't reform ourselves how can we aspire
to reform this benighted country? Labour is now able to
observe the consequences of two concurrent follies: the
flabby pragmatism of 1974–79 and, the reverse of that coin,
the impractical perfectionism of 1979 to 1983. That experience must now facilitate a proper balancing act between the
two dangers implicit in Labour politics. We have much to
fear, but mainly ourselves. The odds are too heavily loaded
against Labour and the building of a better Britain by a
prostituted media utterly subservient to the interests which
control it, an uninformed public, deeply entrenched vested
interests, and a civil service, bank and City which see themselves as the incarnation of national interest, without
compounding all that by our own inadequacies and incompetence. The only true radicalism is that which achieves and
does; not that which asserts and declaims, much as both comfort incompetence.

The real test is one of responsibility. Labour's do not lie to
the activists, the unions or any ideology. They lie to the
people, to a political system which only works for those who
play by its rules and to a nation, relegated now to five more
years of devisive embittering decline at the hands of a
government given a blank mandate to do what it wants
because we distracted attention from its betrayals and evasions on to ourselves. It was all as if the passengers on the
sinking *Titanic* had been distracted from escaping because
the life rafts were the wrong colour, of perverse design, or
had been deliberately holed in the belief that true virtue was
the ability to walk on water.

Labour failed in all these responsibilities. The price of that
failure is paid by the party, weakened and undermined, and
by those it represents and serves. The price of further failure
will be betrayal. Britain in the grip of counter-revolution
needs a strong party of reform. Her people need a party of
betterment. An economy in decline needs the party of the
nation to rebuild the national strength. There is a huge job
to be done and Labour is the only party remotely capable of
doing it, provided it is re-nationalised. The essential pre-condition is that it must become once again the party of the
broad nation, not an introspective, sectarian irrelevancy.

If Labour fails its greatest test it is doomed. The electoral climate is changing, the arena is pitiless and parties, too, obey the laws of evolution: adopt, adapt, improve or be superseded. The function Labour has performed since the war will still need to be fulfilled. If we fail at it someone else will be eager to do it, perhaps not as sincerely or as conscientiously but possibly better if they apply themselves to the serious tasks of a party of change and betterment: carrying the people and winning power. The real problem will be that of transition. In that period politics will be deadlocked, the Conservatives entrenched in power and Britain's last chance, North Sea oil, will be thrown away. God who made us feeble will make us feebler yet.

Index